EMILY DICKINSON'S READINGS OF MEN AND BOOKS

Daguerreotype portrait of Emily Dickinson, 1848 (Amhurst College Library, Massachusetts).

Emily Dickinson's Readings of Men and Books

Sacred Soundings

BENJAMIN LEASE

Professor Emeritus of English
Northeastern Illinois University

First published 1990

Published by
THE MACMILLAN PRESS LTD
Houndmills, Basingstoke, Hampshire RG21 2XS
and London

Companies and representatives
throughout the world

Printed in Hong Kong

British Library Cataloguing in Publication Data
Lease, Benjamin
Emily Dickinson's readings of men and books: sacred soundings.
1. Poetry in English. American writers. Dickinson, Emily, 1830–1886
– Critical studies
I. Title
811'.4
ISBN 0–333–51978–7

Once again, for Mariam

Contents

List of Plates

Following page 76. Thomas Gilbert Dickinson. By permission of the Houghton Library, Harvard University.

Reverend Charles Wadsworth, Courtesy of Office of History, Presbyterian Church (USA).

Samuel Bowles: By permission of the Houghton Library.

Maria Whitney: Northampton Historical Society, Northampton, Massachusetts.

Adjutant Frazar Stearns.

Letter from Emily Dickinson to Thomas Wentworth Higginson, 15 April 1862, by Courtesy of the Trustees of the Boston Public Library.

Colonel Thomas Wentworth Higginson, 1862.

Edward Dickinson, 1874, by permission of the Houghton Library.

Thomas Wentworth Higginson and His Daughter Margaret, 1885: Courtesy of the Jones Library Inc, Amherst, Massachusetts.

Preface

When she was at the point of death, Emily Dickinson wrote her last letter, a two-word message to her beloved Norcross cousins: 'Called back.' Her terse message was the culmination of a lifelong religious quest – a quest centered on the man she called her 'dearest earthly friend', Charles Wadsworth; on the sacred texts she greatly valued (Shakespeare, the Bible, Watts's hymns, the devotional prose and poetry of the seventeenth century); on the man she twice thanked for saving her life, Thomas Wentworth Higginson. Her readings of these men and books are the subject of this book.

Dickinson responded to men and books creatively. She transformed their messages into her own message, the almost eighteen hundred poems that are her legacy to our time. These men (Wadsworth and Higginson) and these books were of crucial importance to her because they spoke most directly to the overriding question she kept asking all of her life: 'Is Immortality True?' Dickinson conveyed in almost all of her poems a religious conviction that was central and unwavering – as it dramatized through numerous personae her rebellious strugglings against rigid orthodoxy. (Carol Johnson's perceptive observation about Donne's faith applies with equal force to Dickinson: 'Doubt is never with Donne the abdication of reason, but the incitement to reason.')

In *Emily Dickinson: A Voice of War*, Shira Wolosky has examined the ways in which the poet's expressions of inner conflict range beyond her private world to reflect the swirling public passions accompanying a terrible war – the ways in which 'The Civil War deeply implicated the whole institution of religion in America'. My book seeks to shed new light on the ways the war transformed the lives and careers of Wadsworth and Higginson – and Dickinson. Wadsworth sent himself into exile (from Philadelphia to San Francisco) because of the war; Higginson left his New England meadows and nature studies for a Southern battleground; Dickinson's poems, written in this time of national crisis, reflect the turbulence in *their* lives as well as in her own.

My book closes with a discussion of Christian Spiritualism, a burgeoning movement in the 1850s when Dickinson was turning to what she regarded to be her sacred vocation. Early in that decade, Edward Hitchcock, a towering religous influence in Amherst, defended mesmerism in a lecture on 'The Telegraphic System of the Universe'; Wadsworth responded, somewhat sympathetically, to the challenge of spiritualist doctrine; Higginson was an ardent advocate all of his life; Dickinson, never an advocate of any doctrine, wrote poems throughout her career that reflected her involvement with the language and imagery of the occult.

The connections between actual events in a poet's life and world and the metaphorical flights of her poems are necessarily tenuous and conjectural. In my attempts to identify and interpret these links, I have proceeded with caution – and have limited my discussion to poems that can be dated, through external evidence, with a considerable degree of accuracy. I will try to demonstrate in the following chapters that the poems of Emily Dickinson have at their center a passionate involvement with family, with friends, with a cultural legacy of rebellion against orthodox answers to the religous questions of her time. (Both Wadsworth and Higginson contributed to that legacy of rebellion.) Her poems continue to speak to us because they are eloquent responses to urgent questions about human existence – questions of vital importance in her life, in her time, in our time.

B. L.

Acknowledgements

Over many years, I owe much to many. I have recorded that indebtedness in the text and notes of this book and want here to thank Richard B. Sewall, the late Thomas H. Johnson, Ralph W. Franklin, Jean McClure Mudge, Albert Gelpi for helpful responses to my inquiries. Others who provided valuable assistance include Mary Louise Pratt, Myron Matlaw, the late Clifford M. Drury, William F. Stapp, Gregory Singleton, Joseph Lease.

The Reverend G. Hall Todd faithfully answered my many questions about Arch Street Presbyterian Church, Philadelphia – and about his close friend, William Scott Wadsworth (son of Emily Dickinson's 'dearest earthly friend', Charles Wadsworth). The Reverend James Gordon Emerson helped me learn more about Calvary Presbyterian Church, San Francisco.

I am much indebted to numerous libraries and their staffs: Northeastern Illinois University Library (with special thanks to Evangeline Mistaras), the Newberry Library, University of Chicago Library, The Presbyterian Historical Society, Jesuit-Kraus-McCormick Library, Northwestern University Library, Garrett Evangelical Library (with special thanks to David Himrod), Seabury-Western Theological Library, the New York Public Library, The Houghton Library of Harvard College Library, the Boston Public Library.

Grateful acknowledgement is made to the following for material reprinted with permission:

Harvard University Press, for material reprinted by permission of the publishers and the Trustees of Amherst College from *The Poems of Emily Dickinson*, edited by Thomas H. Johnson, Cambridge, Mass.: The Belknap Press of Harvard University Press. Copyright 1951, © 1955, 1979, 1983 by the President and Fellows of Harvard College; and for material reprinted by permission of the publishers from *The Letters of Emily Dickinson*, edited by Thomas H. Johnson, Cambridge, Mass.: The Belknap Press of Harvard University Press, Copyright © 1958 by the President and Fellows of Harvard College. © Copyright 1914, 1924, 1932 by Martha Dickinson Bianchi.

Little, Brown and Company for material reprinted from *The Complete Poems of Emily Dickinson*, edited by Thomas H. Johnson. Copyright 1914, 1929, 1935, 1942 by Martha Dickinson Bianchi, copyright renewed © 1957, 1963 by Mary L. Hampson. By permission of Little, Brown and Company.

Poem no. 298, from *Emily Dickinson Face to Face* by Martha D. Bianchi. Copyright 1932 by Martha Dickinson Bianchi. Copyright © renewed 1960 by Alfred Leete Hampson. Reprinted by permission of Houghton Mifflin Company.

Poems no. 1072 and no. 1564, from *Life and Letters of Emily Dickinson* by Martha D. Bianchi. Copyright 1924 by Martha Dickinson Bianchi. Copyright renewed 1952 by Alfred Leete Hampson. Reprinted by permission of Houghton Mifflin Company.

The Trustees of Amherst College for permission to reprint as frontispiece the daguerreotype portrait of Emily Dickinson.

Earl John Clark, my chairman at Northeastern Illinois University, helped in various ways to facilitate my research; Birdie Serlin and Kathryn Snyder provided typing and other assistance.

My book has been improved by suggestions from several readers (some of them anonymous) – and by the encouragement of those who took a personal interest in its evolution: Father Peter J. Powell, Walter Blair, Thomas Savage, Hans-Joachim Lang, David Shapiro, Joseph Lease. My deepest debt is to my wife, Mariam Dubovik Lease, to whom this book is dedicated.

I want, finally, to thank the students in my Dickinson seminars at Northeastern Illinois University for the provocations and illuminations that have spurred me on – that spur me on.

Prologue:
'Immured in Heaven!'

On an April afternoon in 1956, I sat alone in the library of the Homestead, Emily Dickinson's house on Main Street in Amherst, holding in my hands the manuscript of a poem – five short lines signed 'Emily – .' I had telephoned the owner of the house, Mrs Hervey C. Parke, the previous day to ask permission to visit. Mrs Parke gave her consent with some reluctance. I learned the reason for her reluctance only after she had graciously guided me through much of the house, including Emily Dickinson's room. In the second floor hall outside of Lavinia's room, Mrs Parke whispered an apology for not showing it to me: her sister, she explained, was seriously ill and could not be disturbed; I could only marvel at such extraordinary kindness and apologise for my intrusion at such a time.

The manuscript poem Mrs Parke handed me at the close of my tour was encased in celluloid; it had been a gift from the poet's niece, Martha Dickinson Bianchi, to Reverend Parke and his wife, presented to them in 1914 when they took possession of the house. Professor George F. Whicher had examined the poem during one of several visits to the house in the 1930s. Was it, Mrs Parke asked me, one of Emily Dickinson's love poems? She conveyed her displeasure with Professor Whicher's speculations in his biography, *This Was a Poet* (1938), about the poet's love relationship with the Reverend Charles Wadsworth. This is the poem – twenty words, in five short lines:

> Immured in Heaven!
> What a Cell!
> Let every Bondage be,
> Thou sweetest of the Universe,
> Like that which ravished thee!
> (1594)[1]

The idea of being immured (confined within walls, entombed) was puzzling – though heavenly bondage, sweetest of the universe, ravishment, indeed seemed amorous phrases. I had never seen the poem before and puzzlement prevailed; I don't remember how I answered Mrs Parke but suspect that my reply may have been non-committal or, worse, evasive.

I knew that Emily Dickinson loved children but did not learn until later that the manuscript poem Mrs Parke had shown me ('Immured in Heaven!') was indeed a poem about love – a poem about the death of the child she loved most, her eight year-old nephew Gilbert (Gib). It was one of several poems sent over the hedge to the Evergreens to her sister-in-law soon after the sudden death of the boy in October of 1883. Mrs Bianchi (Gilbert's sister) included the poem in *The Single Hound*, the volume of Emily Dickinson's poetry she brought out shortly before presenting the manuscript to the Parkes.

On an afternoon after school in late September of 1883, young Gilbert played with his friend Kendall Emerson in a mud-hole near his house. A few days later he was sick with a fever and on Sunday, 30 September, Austin Dickinson wrote in his diary: 'Gib had a pretty sick night, last, and Sue and I were up with him most of the time.'[2] Several days later, Gilbert's illness was identified as the dread typhoid-malarial fever and by Thursday, 4 October, there was little hope for his recovery. Mabel Loomis Todd wrote in her diary that Austin 'is almost killed by his anxiety and distress . . . ' On the following afternoon, Gilbert died.

The night before his death, Emily Dickinson – accompanied by the family servant Maggie – went over to Austin's house for the first time in fifteen years. She stayed with her beloved nephew until three in the morning, forced to leave when the odor from the disinfectants sickened her; at home, she vomited and went to bed with an anguish and illness from which she never fully recovered.[3] Somehow she rose from her sick bed a few days after Gilbert's death to pencil the following message to Sue, reproduced here in full – for there are few more moving letters in the English language:

Dear Sue –
    The Vision of Immortal Life has been fulfilled –
    How simply at the last the Fathom comes! The Pass-
enger and not the Sea, we find surprises us –
    Gilbert rejoiced in Secrets –
    His Life was panting with them – With what menace of Light he cried "Dont tell, Aunt Emily"! Now my ascended Playmate must instruct *me*. Show us, prattling Preceptor, but the way to thee!

He knew no niggard moment – His Life was full of Boon - The
Playthings of the Dervish were not so wild as his –
No crescent was this Creature – He traveled from the Full –
Such soar, but never set –
I see him in the Star, and meet his sweet velocity in everything
that flies – His Life was like the Bugle, which winds itself away,
his Elegy an echo – his requiem ecstasy –
Dawn and Meridian in one.
Wherefore would he wait, wronged only of Night, which he left
for us –
Without a speculation, our little Ajax spans the whole –

> Pass to thy Rendezvous of Light,
> Pangless except for us –
> Who slowly ford the Mystery
> Which thou hast leaped across!

> Emily.   (L868)

The note sounded here from beginning to end is ecstatic, triumphant
– at what a price we can only surmise for no trace of pain and
suffering is permitted to show. Apocalyptic vision is fused with
personal touches; and the result is overpowering. Gilbert the
child is here – and he who has trimphantly penetrated into
what Emily Dickinson calls elsewhere, in a letter to Judge Lord,
'the "Undiscovered Country"'. The force of the statement "Gilbert
rejoiced in Secrets" resides precisely in the fact that, boylike and
childlike, he loved conspiracy ("Dont tell, Aunt Emily"!). And
simultaneously, effortlessly, the poet is telling us about the greatest
secret that Gilbert, and all of us, rejoice in: boundless life, boundless
vitality. 'No crescent was this Creature – He traveled from the
Full – '[4]
    Richard B. Sewall characterises the letter Emily Dickinson sent
to Sue after Gilbert's death ('The Vision of Immortal Life has been
fulfilled – ') as 'perhaps the finest she ever wrote anybody'; but
beautiful as the letter is, Sewall adds, the grieving mother 'is hardly
in it at all'.[5] It is evident that this extraordinary letter and these
apocalyptic elegies are indeed not conventional expressions of consolation but triumphant outbursts directed as much (if not more) to
the dead boy and Emily Dickinson's own anguish as to the grieving
mother, an anguish distilled, in the poet's alembic, into triumph.
    Thomas Gilbert Dickinson was an exceptional boy whose sudden

death was a grievous blow not only to his family and friends but to the entire town. An obituary notice in the *Amherst Record* tells of a self-reliance in this eight year-old boy 'which seemed somehow to lift him into the sphere of men' – of a quality that drew to him the interest and affection of adults as well as playmates: 'As if by intuition, he found the real stuff of humanity beneath all sorts of garbs and in persons old as well as young . . . ' 'He not only promised much', the notice concludes, 'but he already had provided much'.[6] In her letter to Sue, Dickinson points not to the exceptional insights little Gilbert had in life but to the knowledge he now has in death ('Now my ascended Playmate must instruct *me*'). The poet celebrates an apotheosis; the griefstricken aunt collapses after the death of her beloved nephew.

During Gilbert's brief lifetime, Dickinson wittily enlarged his boyish evasiveness into mythic dimensions: 'Your Urchin is more antique in wiles than the Egyptian Sphinx – ' was her response to his excuses for chasing Vinnie's cat (L664). She transformed a routine school assignment by conveying to Gilbert's teacher a poem about a dead bee's religion playfully celebrating (in Watts's Common Metre) 'the divine Perdition / Of Idleness and Spring – ' while playfully subverting Watts's earnest message about 'Industry and Morals / And every righteous thing' (L712). When Gilbert died, Dickinson made clear her awareness of Sue's suffering: 'The first section of Darkness is the densest, Dear – [she wrote to the bereaved mother] After that, Light trembles in – ' (L874). Her own messages of light for her dead nephew include 'Pass to thy Rendezvous of Light' (1564), 'The Heart has many Doors – ' (1567), 'Expanse cannot be lost – ' (1584), poems that translate grief and loss into moving visions of immortality.

The poem 'Immured in Heaven!' – that Mrs Parke handed to me – was one in the series written and sent to Sue during the terrible days after Gilbert's death. Characteristically, its compressed structure is that of the Isaac Watts hymns that Emily Dickinson grew up with – and drew on for virtually all of her poems. This one is also in Common Metre, alternating eight and six syllables to the line. With a typically free and masterly touch, the poet breaks up the opening eight-syllable line into longer and shorter exclamatory outcries: 'Immured in Heaven! / What a Cell!' The extraordinary bee imagery fuses death and deathlessness: 'The sweetness of honey which the bee gains by ravaging a flower', observes Thomas H. Johnson in his discussion of this poem, ' – a trope which she repeatedly employs in her poems – is also entombed in a cell whose form and shape bear noticeable likeness to a small coffin'.[7] It is also noteworthy that the poet is drawing on the Biblical account of Samson as told in Judges 14 – a story she knew well. In the heavenly bondage of the beloved lost one there is an evocation of honeyed death: God's presence also manifests itself in the riddle that Samson makes out of these extraordinary events – 'Out of the eater came forth meat, and out of the strong came forth sweetness' – and in the marvelous riddle that Dickinson makes of Samson's riddle. And there are other Biblical echoes: Of Peter's bondage and miraculous release (Acts 12:7), of Christ's entombment and Resurrection. All these and more this twenty-word hymn evokes.

What seems evident in all these triumphal elegies on a dead boy is that the woman and the poet mastered life not by rejecting it but by confronting its mystery and challenges with extraordinary intensity, uncompromising directness – and unfailing courage. A poet with the intellectual honesty and emotional intensity of Emily Dickinson, pays a terrible price for facing life, love, death squarely and searchingly – for distilling 'Amazing sense / From ordinary Meanings – ' A tormented woman, soon after the Reverend Dr Charles Wadsworth's death and Judge Lord's dangerous brush with death, after a stroke, asked the Reverend Washington Gladden: 'Is immortality true?'(L752a). Sixteen months later, the poet exulted over little Gilbert's heavenly bondage – and the woman (always more vulnerable than the poet) kept reaching and searching for a lost boy.

All of her life, she kept reaching for the answer to the three-word question she asked Reverend Gladden. To her beloved Judge Lord, she observed: 'On subjects of which we know nothing, . . . we both believe, and disbelieve a hundred times an hour, which keeps Believing nimble' (L750). She rejected easy answers to difficult (or unanswerable) questions – and kept her believing nimble through a lifelong involvement with friends, books (sacred and profane), happenings (private and public). She believed in the light that would tremble in after the densest darkness – for Sue and for herself.

1
A Minister in Exile:
A Minister Remembered

'I had a terror – since September – I could tell to none – ' Emily Dickinson wrote to Thomas Wentworth Higginson in late April of 1862 (L261). The reason for that terror, unspecified in Dickinson's letter and never explained elsewhere, has been the subject of endless speculation – speculation greatly intensified, in 1955, when there came to light the drafts of three letters addressed by the poet to someone she calls 'Master'.[1] Who was this 'Master' – and what part did this person play in the 'terror' that she mentioned to Higginson? Can Dickinson's emotional crisis be linked to the terrible war engulfing the nation during this period?

Among those who have been identified as Master are two of the poet's close friends, Charles Wadsworth and Samuel Bowles – and Otis P. Lord, known to be the poet's lover at a later period; other commentators claim that there is no evidence these letters were ever sent. According to Albert Gelpi, 'It is convincing to read [them] as diary-like addresses to a troubled aspect of herself'. In a recent study centering on Dickinson's ardent relationship with Sue Gilbert (both before and after her marriage to Austin), Martha Nell Smith has similarly suggested that the letters may be imaginative exercises; if they are not fiction, the first two (as dated by Johnson) are probably directed to Sue, the last draft to Judge Lord. In any event, says Smith, our excessive involvement with these letters has obscured our understanding of the poet.[2]

R. W. Franklin, on the other hand, has come to a conclusion that differs sharply from those of Gelpi and Smith: He believes that Master was a man and that 'These three letters . . . stand near the heart of her mystery'. None of the drafts is in a suitable condition to have been posted and there is no evidence that any of them were; but, according to Franklin, they point to 'a long relationship, geographically apart, in which correspondence would have been the primary means of communication'. Dickinson, says Franklin, 'did not write letters as a fictional genre, and these were surely part of a much larger correspondence yet unknown to us' (ML, 5).

Franklin's findings are presented in his new edition of *The Master Letters of Emily Dickinson*, issued at the centennial of the poet's death (in May 1986). His new analysis of the poet's handwriting in the Master letters, part of work in progress involving all the manuscripts, has provided the basis for revising Johnson's order and dates: The first of these letters in Johnson's edition ('I am ill' [L187]) – dated by Johnson in *about 1858* – has been fixed more precisely in *spring 1858*. The order and dates of the next two, the most impassioned and revelatory, are revised more radically: The third of these letters in Johnson's edition ('Oh – did I offend it' [L248]) has been found by Franklin to be the second, with the date changed from *early 1862?* to *early 1861*; the second of these letters in Johnson's edition ('If you saw a bullet' [L233]) has been found by Franklin to be the third, with the date fixed more precisely from *about 1861* to *summer 1861* (ML, 7–9).

The new dates assigned by Franklin to the most emotional of the Master letters coincide with an upheaval, in early 1861 and the summer of 1861, in Charles Wadsworth's life as a minister (discussed later in this chapter). We may never know with certainty to whom these letters were directed – or whether they were actually sent. There are, however, new reasons to believe that the crisis in Dickinson's emotional life reflected in the Master letters may be linked to a crisis in Wadsworth's life.

Our knowledge about the Dickinson–Wadsworth relationship is sketchy and can be briefly summarised: Dickinson visited Philadelphia in March 1855 and probably heard Wadsworth preach; in March 1860 the minister visited her in Amherst; in April 1862 he left Philadelphia to become pastor of Calvary Church, San Francisco; there are evidences of an extensive Dickinson–Wadsworth correspondence (now lost) – though only one undated Wadsworth letter, formally pastoral in tone, has survived; in August 1880, Wadsworth again visited the poet in Amherst; after Wadsworth's death, his closest friends initiated a correspondence with her – and she wrote about the minister at length in numerous letters, referring to him as 'My closest earthly friend' and 'My Shepherd from "Little Girl"hood' (L765 and L766). Though slender, the evidence surrounding their friendship deserves renewed attention – and should not be obscured or overshadowed by melodramatic accounts of the relationship.[3] Charles Wadsworth was Emily Dickinson's most highly valued religious guide and what she considered to be her sacred vocation is illuminated by the ways in which she responded to his message.

1

Emily Dickinson's childhood and young womanhood revolved around the orthodox village piety she experienced in the First Church of Christ, in the Amherst Academy, and in the Mount Holyoke Female Seminary. She attended church services fairly regularly until she was thirty. About one sermon, delivered in 1853 by the Reverend Edwards Amasa Park, she wrote to her brother Austin with unrestrained enthusiasm:

> I never heard anything like it, and dont expect to again, till we stand at the great white throne . . . . The students and chapel people all came, to our church, and it was very full, and still – so still, the buzzing of a fly would have boomed like a cannon. And when it was all over, and that wonderful man sat down, people stared at each other, and looked as wan and wild, as if they had seen a spirit, and wondered they had not died. (L142)

Though a fairly regular churchgoer, and occasionally enthusiastic about sermons and the ministers who delivered them, she could not – despite the waves of religious revivalism that periodically engulfed the village – bring herself to a declaration of faith and to membership in the Church. A personal experience of God's grace was a prerequisite and most of her friends and all the members of her family responded – except for Emily. 'Christ is calling everyone here', she wrote a friend in April of 1850, 'all of my companions have answered, even my darling Vinnie believes she loves, and trusts him, and I am standing alone in my rebellion, and growing very careless'. She marvels, perhaps a shade ironically, on the great change that has taken place among her friends who have found Christ ('their voices are kind, and gentle, and the tears fill their eyes so often, I really think I envy them') and she asks her friends to pray 'that the hand may be held to me, and I may be led away' (L35).

A part of her continued to hold fast to the conventional village pieties; but a larger part rebelled – and continued to rebel as long as she lived – against the easy answers these provided. 'You are growing wiser than I am', she wrote to a friend and former classmate when she was twenty, and nipping in the bud fancies which I let blossom – perchance to bear no fruit, or if plucked, I may find it bitter. The shore is safer, Abiah, but I love to buffet the sea – I can count the bitter wrecks here in these pleasant waters, and hear the murmuring winds, but oh, I love the danger! You are learning control and firmness. Christ Jesus will love you more. I'm afraid he don't love me *any*! (L39)

This is the voice not of a disbeliever but of one unable to surrender her own 'fancies' – her free-ranging explorations of religious concerns.

She could toy with the idea of Unitarianism in a poem (copied about 1862) that created shock waves in Boston when it was published posthumously three decades later:

> God is a distant – stately Lover –
> Woos, as He states us – by His son –
> Verily, a Vicarious Courtship –
> "Miles", and "Priscilla", were such an One –
>
> But, lest the Soul – like fair "Priscilla"
> Choose the Envoy – and spurn the Groom –
> Vouches, with hyperbolic archness –
> "Miles", and "John Alden" were Synonyme –
>   (357)

She stood apart from the other members of the village in her audacity and wit – in her rejection of orthodox answers to the religious questions she was determined to answer for herself.

2

It was this toughminded and resolutely determined 'irreverence' that drew her to the Reverend Charles Wadsworth. He was an overpowering preacher whose force was conveyed less by vehement gesture or theatrical mannerism than by a moral intensity that penetratred hearts usually unsusceptible to sermon oratory.[4] And there was another side to Wadsworth that was equally appealing: his playfulness and wit. Mark Twain (whose humor was, in many ways, anticipated by or – since they were contemporaries – independently expressed by Emily Dickinson) heard Wadsworth preach in San Francisco and left a vivid record of the minister's deadpan humour:

> Dr. Wadsworth never fails to preach an able sermon; but every now and then, with an admirable assumption of not being aware of it, he will get off a firstrate joke and then frown severely at any one who is surprised into smiling at it . . . . Several people there on Sunday suddenly laughed and as suddenly stopped again, when he gravely gave the Sunday School books a blast and spoke of 'the good little boys in them who always went to heaven, and the bad little boys who infallibly got drowned on Sunday,' and then swept a savage frown around the house and blighted every smile in the congregation.[5]

Emily Dickinson knew well and loved what she called his 'inscrutable roguery' – for she possessed it in good measure herself. And she also knew well the dark side of 'my Philadelphia' – as she referred to him shortly after his death (L750). 'My life is full of dark secrets', Wadsworth told her on one occasion (L776); she touched on some of these secrets in an extensive correspondence initiated by Wadsworth's closest friends, the Clark brothers (discussed later in this chapter).

At the Arch Street Church, where Emily Dickinson first heard Wadsworth preach, the minister was both magnetic and mystifying. He was cordial and playfully witty among his special friends – but strangely diffident and reserved toward his parishioners: His pulpit was so located that he could enter and leave it through the basement of the building without the usual greetings and social interaction that follow a sermon. This reserve also characterised his behavior outside the church; to avoid a casual encounter and conversation, he would cross the street.[6]

Lavinia Dickinson dutifully burned the letters received by her sister from Wadsworth and other correspondents. One brief note, undated – possibly sent a year or two after Emily Dickinson heard him preach – has survived. Though unsigned, it is in Wadsworth's handwriting and on stationery embossed with his initials; he is responding to a troubled communication from her:

My Dear Miss Dickenson

I am distressed beyond measure at your note, received this moment, – can only imagine the affliction which has befallen, or is now befalling you.

Believe me, be what it may, you have all my sympathy, and my constant, earnest prayers.

I am very, very anxious to learn more definitely of your trial – and though I have no right to intrude upon your sorrow yet I beg you to write me, though it be but a word.

In great haste
Sincerely and most
Affectionately *Yours* —

[L248a]

We do not know what crisis Emily Dickinson was undergoing – but her reaching out in her trouble to Wadsworth in Philadelphia testifies to the depth of her feeling for the minister.

3

It is uncertain what sermon she heard in Philadelphia – or what sermons were mailed to her by the Coleman family, her hosts during her visit there. Indications of Wadsworth's tremendous appeal, however, may be readily gleaned from 'The Gospel Call', a characteristic sermon delivered at the Arch Street Church on 11 April 1858. An extended passage may serve to illustrate Wadsworth's passionate preaching style – and his irresistible appeal to Emily Dickinson:

Oh, what a call is this! The Spirit and the Bride call, and he that heareth calls . . . . And the Church below, Christ's witness unto the world, in all her ordinances and utterances, cries, "Come, come!"and the Church above, with the rustling of white robes, and the sweeping of golden harps, cries, "Come, come!" And the angels of heaven, lo! rank above rank, the immortal Principalities, as they circle the eternal throne, they have caught up the sound, and cry, "Come, come!" . . . *"And the Spirit and the Bride say, Come; and let him that heareth say, Come; and let him that is athirst come*, and whosoever will, let him take the water of life freely!"[7]

Wadsworth's text, quoted at the conclusion, is Revelation 22:17 – a passage Emily Dickinson knew and loved. (She quotes from it in an 1851 letter to Austin; and she cites this book of the Bible in a letter to Thomas Wentworth Higginson, the only one thus singled out.)

Is it a direct response to Wadsworth's sermon or an independent response that reveals their spiritual kinship when she writes (in a poem copied about 1862):

> Me – come! My dazzled face
> In such a shining place!
> Me – hear! My foreign Ear
> The sounds of Welcome – there!
>
> The Saints forget
> Our bashful feet –
>
> My Holiday, shall be
> That They – remember me –
> My Paradise – the fame
> That They – pronounce my name –
>   (431)

Dickinson's vision of a heaven in which she will be greeted by name parallels that offered by Wadsworth in another sermon (that quotes from Revelation 21:27), 'The Mortal Immortalized': 'The very *names* God's children bear on earth are written in the Lamb's Book of Life, and shall be theirs as well in "the many mansions" forever.' In 'Me – come! My dazzled face', Dickinson echoes Revelation and, possibly, Wadsworth – but the colloquial touches are distinctive ('Me – Come!' / Me hear!'); and the sonorities of scripture and sermon oratory are replaced by the exultant outcries of a private self surprised by glory.[8]

Other sermons – perhaps sent to her by the minister or friends – help us better understand Wadsworth and his powerful hold over the mind and heart of Emily Dickinson. The preacher conveyed a special eloquence when dealing with the subject of holy communion – the sacrament of the Lord's Supper. *The Imitation of Christ* of Thomas à Kempis, a devotional work of special importance to the poet, dwelled on the central importance and efficacy of Communion.[9] Wadsworth's emphasis on liturgical worship reflected, to some extent, the eucharistic revival in the Presbyterian Church – a revival vigorously opposed by some Old School ministers who saw it as a return to Anglican and papist doctrine. Wadsworth avoided the extreme approach of his controversial contemporary John W. Nevin (who argued that 'the Eucharist forms the very heart of the whole Christian worship')[10]—but a passage from the sermon 'Self-Knowledge', delivered at the Arch Street Church in 1860, reflects Wadsworth's affinities with those advocating the special efficacy of the Lord's Supper:

> We have come from the communion. We are therefore re-consecrate! And we feel to-day that such reconsecration was due unto our Saviour. Oh, "he was bruised for our iniquity!" We saw it. We felt it! That *"body"* – the body of the Incarnate God, – was *"broken"* for our iniquity. That *"blood,"* that mysterious blood of an Incarnate God, was *"shed"* for our iniquity! Here, here, were unto us the memorials of a divine consecration! All the works of God, all the riches of God, all the attributes of God, all the persons of God, *consecrated unto us!* "All things present" – this universal range and power of the economy of Providence; "All things to come" – all that higher economy of the eternal world – thrones, crowns, white robes, heavenly mansions – all – all consecrate to us! God having given them to be ours, and using them henceforth for our good and glory.[11]

The reenactment of the stages of Christ's sacrifice as 'memorials of a divine consecration' separates Wadsworth from Nevin's belief in 'an actual union' on the part of the worshiper with 'the Saviour's glorified body'; but his impassioned eloquence and imagery ('We saw it. We felt it!') establish his kinship with Nevin – and with Emily Dickinson's passionate involvement with Thomas à Kempis.

Another sermon by Wadsworth places him even closer to Emily Dickinson – and at a greater distance from the austere reasoning of both camps in the liturgical controversy that surrounded him. For 'Communion', Wadsworth takes verses from The Song of Solomon as his text: *"My beloved has gone down into his garden, to the bed of spices, to feed in the garden, and to gather lilies. I am my beloved's and my beloved is mine"* (6:2, 3). This is a book, the minister observes, 'which no profane hand should ever be permitted to open, and which no profane hand should be permitted to close'. This sacrament of communion as set forth in this glorious book makes visible Christ's pleasure in the believer, the believer's pleasure in Christ: 'The picture is of an Oriental garden, wherein walk two loving spirits, joyously conversing, while they partake of its delicious fruits . . . . ' Those who partake of the fruit in this garden are refreshed and renewed by the heavenly voice of our Saviour 'filling all the soul, and thy banner over us Love – Love!'[12]

But it was Wadsworth's way with words, his manner of delivery, that was as compelling to Emily Dickinson as his message. A tribute to his pulpit oratory by a fellow minister praises Wadsworth in terms that convey his kinship to the poet:

> He finds the hidden manna in abundance [wrote Reverend George Burrowes in 1863] where others do not suspect even its existence. Where other men would pass without casting even a glance at portions of Scripture deemed useless and dead as the body of the slain lion, he, like Samson, "turning aside to see the carcase," finds these dead ceremonies . . . swarming with truths . . . , from which he brings forth . . . that which is "sweet to the taste, sweeter than honey and the honey-comb."

Burrowes compares Wadsworth to Shakespeare in his gift for transforming metaphysical truths into living reality. And – though he did not know of her existence – he praises Wadsworth in terms applicable to Emily Dickinson. The minister, says Burrowes, sets forth his thought 'with a powerful condensation, till it glows like a diamond'; he distills into a single sentence the equivalent of a laborious argument; his irony and wit are overpowering: 'Like lightning from a clear sky, when least expected there is a flash and a smash' – and 'the empty fooleries of the day' are totally pulverised.[13]

4

The first of the Master Letters, dated by Franklin in the spring of 1858, expresses the wish that she were an artist gifted enough to create for him, in 'God's house', what Michelangelo did for the Pope in his house (the Sistine Chapel); she is grieved to learn of his illness, is herself ill – but at her door there are the sights and sounds of springtime:

> I would that all I love, should be weak no more. The Violets are by my side – the Robin very near – and "Spring" – they say, Who is she – going by the door -
> Indeed it is God's house – and these are gates of Heaven, and to and fro, the angels go, with their sweet postillions – I wish that I were great, like Mr – Michael Angelo, and could paint for you. (ML, 12–15)

Several months earlier, in January, a friend had sent her a Wadsworth sermon, possibly 'Religious Glorying'.[14] In her first Master letter, Dickinson's angels moving to and fro seem to echo a passage in 'The Gospel Call', a sermon delivered by Wadsworth on 11 April: 'The Spirit and the Bride call . . . And the angels of heaven . . . circle the eternal throne . . . . '[15]

In her own way, she was beginning to do for her Master what Michelangelo did for the Pope; it was during this year that she began to copy out her poems and gather them into fascicles. She seems to be responding, in the letter to her Master, to his puzzlement about a poem she has sent to him: 'You ask me what my flowers said – then they were disobedient – I gave them messages – They said what the lips in the West, say, when the sun goes down, and so says the Dawn –' (ML, 15–16) The poem cannot be readily identified; among several poems, dated in 1858, with flowers as subject, 'The gentian weaves her fringes' (18) is a possible candidate.

Several months after his mother's death on 1 October 1859, the Reverend Dr Charles Wadsworth came to Amherst to see Emily Dickinson. She inquired about the black band in his hat and he told her about his loss; 'Did you love her', she asked – and he replied 'with his deep "Yes"' (L773). Dickinson's extensive correspondence with the Clark brothers, during the last years of her life, sheds important light on her relationship with the minister whom she called her 'dearest earthly friend'. Even more revealing are the two impassioned 'Master' letter drafts of 1861 – and, in late 1861 and early 1862, her extraordinary exchange of letters (the result of an extraordinary misunderstanding) with another minister, the Reverend Edward S. Dwight. These revelations are best examined in the light of the great crisis threatening the life of the nation during this fateful time.

5

In one of her many letters to James D. Clark after Wadsworth's death, Emily Dickinson told of the minister's reference – in a letter or during a visit – to his son '"Willie", whom, forgive me the arrogance, he told me was like me – though I, not knowing "Willie", was benighted still' (L776). This was William Scott Wadsworth, born in San Francisco in 1868, and named after the Reverend William Anderson Scott, founder (in 1855) and first pastor of Calvary Presbyterian Church in San Francisco – until his resignation on 1 July 1861 (temporarily withdrawn until mob action at the church in September forced him out of the pulpit and the city). Charles Wadsworth's great admiration for Dr Scott, reflected in the name he gave his son, seems to have been occasioned by a friendship initiated in the late 1850s; they may have met during the three successive years (1858, 1859, 1860) Scott was ministerial commissioner to the Old School General Assemblies in Philadelphia. After resigning in July 1861, Scott may have asked his friend to consider a call from Calvary Church as his successor; their friendship probably contributed to Wadsworth's being chosen to replace Scott at a meeting of the congregation on 9 December 1861 – a selection that may have been preceded by overtures as early as July.[16]

A native of Tennessee, William Anderson Scott proclaimed pro-Confederate sentiments that increasingly antagonised townspeople and his own congregants – who, though predominantly Southern, could not support secession. In February 1861, after the inauguration of Jefferson Davis as President of the Confederacy, Scott invoked divine blessings 'upon the Presidents and Vice Presidents of both Confederacies'. Mounting troubles with his congregation led to his resignation in July; he withdrew his resignation for a time – but tensions increased to intolerable levels throughout the summer. In early August, two Presbyterian periodicals in the East published erroneous reports that Scott's resignation had been accepted. In mid-September, Scott denounced the decision of the Presbytery of California to speak out against the Southern rebellion and lend full support to the federal government: 'Jefferson Davis is no usurper [said Scott]; he is as much a President as Abraham Lincoln is.' The response was outrage ('Dr Scott in his presbytery stands alone [said one of his opponents]; left alone even by his own church'). After mob violence at Calvary Church on Sunday, 22 September, Dr Scott's resignation was resubmitted and finally accepted – and, on 1 October, he and his family precipitously left San Francisco for a two-year exile in Europe.[17]

The year of crisis, 1861, opened with a 'Day of Humiliation and Prayer' (on Friday, 4 January) proclaimed by President Buchanan – and Dr Wadsworth preached a sermon on our 'great national peril'. (Lincoln's election had precipitated the crisis; South Carolina had just seceded from the Union.) The evil, Wadsworth argued, was not slavery but a 'self-righteous hypocrisy' about slavery – about which we should have no more concern 'than with Russian serfdom'. He cited Scripture in support of his view that the institution of slavery was not in itself a sin in God's eyes. Our greatest sin, he claims, has been the wicked and hypocritical assaults 'launched against our Christian brethren of the South'; he is thoroughly convinced that 'in all the unscrupulous and persistent evil speaking the world has ever known there has been nothing to compare with the malignant misrepresentation our Southern brethren have received at the hands of nominal Christians at the north'. This hostile and hypocritical spirit of self-righteousness is growing, has 'broken in two the great Christian denominations of the Church' and 'brought us this day . . . upon the very verge of national destruction'. The sermon concludes with an extended plea for genuine repentance and 'exalting faith'.[18]

A prefatory exchange of letters reproduced in the printed version of Wadsworth's sermon makes it clear that 'The undersigned [thirteen] members of your congregation' earnestly subscribe to its sentiments. But the congregation of the Arch Street Church was as deeply divided on this issue as the Presbyterian Church itself – and the nation. An indication of the deep divisions that existed within individual congregations, especially in the North, is the fact that the Arch Street Church congregation – consisting predominantly of Northerners – did not install as Wadsworth's successor the interim minister Dr William Swann Plummer, who also believed that slavery was Biblically sanctioned, but eventually turned to a native Ohioan, Nathaniel W. Conklin, who apparently held acceptable anti-slavery views.[19] During the spring, summer and fall of 1861, Dr Wadsworth – and the thirteen members of the congregation who shared his views on slavery – seem to have been increasingly in the minority;[20] but despite his Southern sympathies, Wadsworth gave unqualified support to the Union cause after the outbreak of hostilities.

With the firing on Fort Sumter and the outbreak of the Civil War, Wadsworth threw his support to the imperilled Union. In a sermon delivered in May 1861, Wadsworth announced that 'this emphatically is "a good fight"' – that 'the Christian should prove himself pre-eminently "*a good soldier of Christ Jesus*"'. In his Thanksgiving Day sermon that year, however – shortly before an official confirmation of his call to Calvary Church – the patriotic note is less strident; the war is seen as a great ordeal ordained by God, an ordeal that is preparing us for a greater good: 'God seems to be treating us as he treated Israel' but it will some day 'be seen that this our Exodus, like the old, was the very richest in the experience of God's loving wisdom . . . . '[21] The call from Calvary Church – with its predominantly Southern congregation (and its predominantly pro-Union sentiment) – must have been both a bitter and welcome one.

Wadsworth had served faithfully and well in Philadelphia since 1850 and San Francisco was remote and incaccessible. But even more remote and inaccessible than San Francisco to Wadsworth must have seemed the hearts of most of his own Arch Street Church congregants – members of his flock who found it impossible to share their minister's view of slavery. He thought of himself as God's servant preaching truths about slavery that came to him from God. He did not find it possible to repudiate the General Assembly (that had repudiated *his* God-given views) and ally himself with the Southern Presbyteries; instead, he accepted the call from Calvary Church and went into what could be called a self-imposed exile. In Shakespeare's tragedy *Richard II*, Richard is 'God's substitute, / His deputy anointed in His sight' (I.ii.37–8); in one of the poems of royal suffering and transcendent union that Emily Dickinson wrote during this period, her persona speaks as 'Empress of Calvary', a partner to the sovereignty and sacred suffering of her monarch. That partnership was integrally linked to her sacred vocation as a poet.

Shortly before Wadsworth's departure for San Francisco, Dickinson sent a letter to Samuel Bowles that consisted of the poem 'Title divine – is mine!' – and an appended plea:

> Title divine – is mine!
> The Wife – without the Sign!
> Acute Degree – conferred on me –
> Empress of Calvary!
> Royal – all but the Crown!
> Betrothed – without the swoon
> God sends us Women –
> When you – hold – Garnet to Garnet –
> Gold – to Gold –
> Born – Bridalled – Shrouded –
> In a Day –
> "My Husband" – women say –
> Stroking the Melody –
> Is *this* – the way?
>
> Here's – what I had to "tell you" –
> You will tell no other? Honor – is it's
> own pawn –
>   (L250)

The closing sentence about honour's pawn was repeated in the momentous first letter she wrote to Higginson a few weeks later – the letter asking whether the four enclosed poems were 'alive'. This link between the two communications lends support to Karen A. Dandurand's view that 'Title divine – is mine!' is a statement to Bowles about her need not to publish her poems rather than an autobiographical confession about her 'mystical marriage'.[22] I would urge, however, that an announcement about her status as a private poet is no less autobiographical than one about a mystical marriage; and I would suggest, further, that her new status in her sacred vocation is an important dimension of – not an alternative to – her new status as 'the Wife – without the Sign!' This is not to say that this and numerous other poems in this vein can and should be read as literal autobiographical statements; but their metaphorical references are illuminated by what she had written earlier in letters to her Master: Her wish, expressed in the spring of 1858, 'that I were great, like Mr – Michael Angelo, and could paint for you'; her 'love of the – Plantagenet', conveyed in the summer of 1861—a love that makes irrepressible her wish 'that mine were the Queen's place – ' (ML, 15, 35–6).

By the early 1860s – about the time of the Reverend Wadsworth's departure for San Francisco and his new pastorate at Calvary Church – Emily Dickinson began dressing exclusively in white ('Mine – by the Right of the White Election!'[528]) and to announce (in her poems) a royal and mystical marriage ('Title divine – is mine!/ . . . Empress of Calvary!' [1072]). In Thomas à Kempis' *The Imitation of Christ* she found a model for combating 'lukewarmness of spirit' through a daily regimen free of superficial distraction that permits the cloistered one to penetrate the essential 'things eternal'; there are few truly contemplative men, the *Imitation* proclaims, 'because few have the knowledge to withdraw themselves fully from perishing creatures'.[23] 'The Queen Recluse' – as Samuel Bowles jocularly referred to her (in a letter to Austin in 1863) – withdrew herself increasingly and successfully from most 'perishing creatures'.

6

The second Master letter that has survived, dated by Franklin in early 1861, centers on Emily Dickinson's state of mind: her anguish over the anger she has aroused in her beloved; her overpowering need to retain an important place in his life.

'Oh – did I offend it – ' she begins her letter, '[Did'nt it want me to tell it the truth]'. She pleads pardon for having grieved her Lord: ' . . . perhaps her odd – Backwoodsman [life] ways [troubled] teased his finer (sense) nature –' She reminds him of her careful refusal to show her pain and suffering during 'that awful parting' – but also informs him that the 'Tomahawk in my side' is less hurtful than the pain she is now feeling ('Her Master stabs her more – '). She pleads with her 'Master' to 'open your life wide and take [in] me in forever . . . . ' She will be glad to be his 'best little girl', never 'noisy' and troublesome. She assures him that 'nobody else will see me, but you – but that is enough – I shall not want any more – and all that Heaven will . . . only disappoint me – because . . . it's not so dear' (ML, 22–9). The subservience of this desperate pleading has troubled some critics; but it is, as Sandra Gilbert and Susan Gubar have pointed out, a subservience accompanied by a human despair and a poet's strength: 'Mothered by Awe, [Dickinson] . . . might sometimes abase herself to her distant Master in a fever of despair, but she could also transform him into a powerful muse who served *her* purposes.'[24]

Several months later, she writes again to her Master in a letter that focuses not only on her own suffering and need but also on the trouble that *he* is experiencing. Franklin has dated this letter in the summer of 1861 on the basis of a new analysis of Dickinson's handwriting; and a change that she made in her draft-letter provides Franklin with additional evidence. She first wrote: 'I want to see you more – Sir – than all I wish for in this world – and the wish – altered a little – will be my only one – for the skies – Could you come to New England – this summer – could you come to Amherst – Would you like to come – Master?' She then crossed out 'this summer' – perhaps as too impatient and insistent; this cancellation points to the likelihood, Franklin suggests, 'that she was referring to the season at hand' (ML, 8–9). The season at hand, the summer of 1861, was a troubled one for the Reverend Dr Charles Wadsworth – and there are detailed references in Dickinson's letter that point toward the fact that the man she called her 'dearest earthly friend' may also be the man she called 'Master'.

The letter opens with a powerful trope: 'If you saw a bullet hit a Bird – and he told you he was'nt shot – you might weep at his courtesy, but you would certainly doubt his word – ' She seems to be responding to questions he has raised about the intensity and permanence of her love: 'One drop more from the gash that stains your Daisy's bosom – then would you *believe?'* God made her and 'built the heart' in her. She had asked her Master for "Redemption" but he had given her something else. She cannot repress – try as she will – her wish to be at his side, to share his royal presence as Queen of the Plantagenet. He has emphatically forbidden her to 'come nearer than Presbyteries – and nearer than the new Coat – that the Tailor made – ' And he has forbidden 'the prank of the Heart at play on the Heart – in holy Holiday – 'He has asked her to explain what it is she needs ("Tell you of the want") and can only compare her limitless need to a leech on her tiny arm – and to the horizon and the sea. She does not know what he can do for that need – but if they suddenly exchanged bodies,[25] and he (transformed) 'cared so for me' (transformed), would he still be as indifferent to her fate: 'Could you forget me in fight, or flight – or the foreign land?' There was a time, she continues, when she thought that death would bring them together ('so I died as fast as I could') – and she now knows that the "Corporation" are going too – so [Eternity] Heaven wont be sequestered – [at all] now – ' She closes her letter with the impassioned plea that he come to New England, to Amherst, this summer (ML, 32–43).

In May of 1861, the General Assembly of the Presbyterian Church met in Philadelphia soon after the firing on Fort Sumter and the outbreak of the Civil War; after a bitter debate, a resolution was adopted announcing its support of the Federal Government 'in the spirit of that Christian patriotism which the Scriptures enjoin, and which has always characterized this Church . . . . ' That summer and fall, 'forty-seven Southern presbyteries severed their relationship with the Old School General Assembly' – and William Anderson Scott's tenure at Calvary Church became increasingly precarious.[26] Wadsworth, though a Union supporter, sympathized strongly with the Southern stand on slavery, a position that made him more acceptable to the preponderantly Southern congregants of Calvary Church than to the members of his own Arch Street Church. By late summer, Scott had offered to resign several times – and seems to have turned to his friend Wadsworth as a possible successor. And Wadsworth may have conveyed this possibility to Emily Dickinson.

Several cryptic details in Dickinson's letter to her Master are clarified when they are examined in the light of Wadsworth's crisis during this turbulent time: 'Could you forget me in fight, or flight – or the foreign land?' pithily summarizes his controversial position in the nation and in his church – and refers to his imminent move a continent away; when Samuel Bowles visited California in 1865, his biographer observed that 'New York was farther from San Francisco than it is to-day [1885] from Constantinople'.[27]

The reference to 'Presbyteries' playfully suggests that his ruling elders – and his new coat – are closer to him and his heart than she can ever be. Dickinson's reference to 'the "Corporation" . . . going' to heaven too – puzzling to commentators who have taken note of it – echoes a term frequently used in relation to the Presbyterian Church – a term richly suggestive of medieval concepts of Christian kingship and church polity. 'He [Christ] doth . . . incorporate all christen folke and hys owne bodye together in one corporacyon mistical', wrote Sir Thomas More in his *Treatise on the Passion*; in Elizabethan England, it was a commonplace that the king 'is a Corporation in himself that liveth ever'. Kingship and the body of the Church (incorporating Christ's body) were fused in mystical union; and in those countries in which there was separation of State and Church, there was a tendency, especially pronounced in mid-nineteenth century America, for 'the Churches [to] form private corporations'.[28] (Dickinson's lexicon quotes Blackstone in describing a *corporation aggregate* as consisting of, among others, 'the dean and chapter of a cathedral church'; Blackstone says further that 'A *corporation sole* consists of one person only and his successors, as a king or a bishop'.) She can find refuge with her Master in heaven for 'the "Corporation"' will join them there – and 'Heaven wont be sequestered – [at all] now – ' (ML, 40). Here she is playing with the double meaning of *sequester*: 'To seclude . . . ; to keep apart from society'; or, in ecclesiastical terms, 'to excommunicate'.[29] Their celestial reunion would be in a heaven sacred to his church; and if he came to Amherst this summer, it would do no harm – for they both fear God (ML, 43).[30]

The turbulent events related to the war were swirling about both pulpits – in the Arch Street and Calvary Presbyterian Churches – and were also reaching out to Amherst at the time, probably early August, this Master letter was written. This last of the three surviving letter-drafts written by Dickinson to her Master points persuasively toward Charles Wadsworth. If the minister was indeed the Master, did he come to New England, to Amherst, that summer? We cannot know for certain – but we now know that the terror 'since September – I could tell to none – ' is almost certainly rooted in the reality of Wadsworth's imminent flight.

A poem enclosed in the letter to Higginson telling of her terror may have been written soon after her impassioned plea to her Master to come to her: 'There came a Day – at Summer's full' (322) tells of a day that brought sacramental union ('Each was to each The Sealed Church, / Permitted to commune this – time – '); and it was also a day of 'awful parting' ('So faces on two Decks, look back, / Bound to opposing lands – ') – a day that first pointed, beyond the grave, 'To that new Marriage, / Justified – through Calvaries of Love – ' This powerful poem may, of course, be nothing more than a poetic flight of fancy about a meeting and parting that never actually took place. But it seems likely that the poem – if it cannot be linked to an actual meeting – can be linked to an actual request for such a meeting. Her Master's crisis – his 'fight' and imminent 'flight' – seems to illuminate 'There came a Day – ' in somewhat the same way that Gilbert's death illuminates 'Immured in Heaven!'[31]

The turbulent relationship between Emily Dickinson and her Master was further shaken, during the closing weeks of 1861 and opening weeks of the new year, by an unpredictable development – a development in which the poem 'There came a Day – ' played a significant part.

7

The Amherst minister she found most persuasive and whose personality was most congenial was the Reverend Edward S. Dwight; she had turned to him as a friend and counselor during the late 1850s. In 1860, because of his wife's failing health (she was suffering from pulmonary tuberculosis), Dwight resigned his pastorate and resettled in Gorham, Maine. After Mrs Dwight's death, in September of 1861, Emily Dickinson sent a note of sympathy and – in mid-December (overwhelmed by her own troubles) – a warm letter recalling her comforting visits to Reverend Dwight's study and her friendship and correspondence with his dead wife ('I held them [her letters] to my lips – . . . and then the tears fell so – I feared that they would blot them out – ' [L243]). But, through a strange (and not so strange) blunder, this letter of condolence was sealed into an envelope possibly addressed to Wadsworth; and a letter that may have been intended for Wadsworth was instead sent to Dwight.

'I made the mistake – ' she wrote to Dwight on 2 January 1862,

– and was just about to recall the note – *misenveloped* to you –
and *your's* – to the other friend – which I just knew – when my
"Sister's" face – put this world from mine – nor should I mention
it – except the familiar address – must have surprised your taste
– I have the friend who loves me – and thinks me larger than I
am – and to reduce a Glamour, innocently caused – I sent the little
Verse to *Him*. Your gentle answer – undeserved, I more thank you
for. (L246)

Her 'other friend' had apparently just informed her of the
misenveloping mistake (' – which I just knew – '); how else
could she have come to know she had reversed the contents of
the envelopes posted a few weeks before? And her response to
Dwight's letter (his letter has not survived) makes it clear that
the mistake had been compounded: Dwight was writing under the
mistaken impression that the misenveloped letter had actually been
intended for him.

She had enclosed a poem and now finds it necessary to explain
that 'I sent the little Verse to *Him*' (her 'other friend'). Dwight
apparently did not enclose the misenveloped letter because of this
misunderstanding – but he does enclose a photograph of his dead
wife ('My little Sister's face – so dear – so unexpected') and a poem
of his own ('Dear friend – I read the verse – '). She tactfully clears
up any misapprehensions he might have about her feelings for him
– and tells him he is mistaken when he says of the portrait he has
pointedly enclosed of his wife that it 'might remind me of my
former friend' ('if you please – I remember *more* – and *not* "less"
– as you said').

Dwight's troubled response and enclosure of his dead wife's
portrait to remind Emily Dickinson of her former friend is understandable – and somewhat suggestive of Restoration Comedy. But
there seems also to have been more serious repercussions from this
misenveloping mishap. A recently widowed minister receives a
declaration of love; and a minister whose wife was very much alive
(for Wadsworth seems likely to have been 'the other friend') receives
a letter of condolence over her death – with tender expressions of
affection for him, for his dead wife, for his children. Wadsworth
– unlike Dwight – would have immediately understood what he
had received: A letter from Emily Dickinson intended for someone
else. But he would also immediately understand something else:
Someone else had received a letter from Emily Dickinson intended

for him. By this time, Wadsworth was committed to his decision to leave Philadelphia for San Francisco and Calvary Church; this episode may have removed any remaining doubts about accepting the call.

Her letter to Reverend Dwight explaining her error and conveying her love for his dead wife closed with an excerpt from 'There came a Day at Summer's full – '. The closing stanza of this poem dwells, as do a number of other poems written at this time and during this terrible year, on the word *Calvary* – and on the Passion that the poem's persona and the lover from whom she must part are experiencing. It is illuminating to set the original version alongside the version she adapted to the memory of Dwight's dead wife:

[Original version]

> Sufficient troth, that we shall rise –
> Deposed – at length, the Grave –
> To that new Marriage,
> Justified – through Calvaries of Love –
> (322)

[Version adapted for Dwight]

> Sufficient troth – that she will rise –
> Deposed – at last – the Grave –
> To that *new* fondness – Justified –
> by Calvaries of love –
> (L246)

No record has survived of Dwight's reaction to Emily Dickinson's letter of explanation – and their corespondence seems at this point to break off permanently.

A few months later she informed Higginson of the 'terror – since September – I could tell to none – and so I sing, as the Boy does by the Burying Ground – because I am afraid – ' (L261). But though she did not tell all, she did find one to whom she could tell something of her terror – one who helped her survive this period of great suffering: Samuel Bowles. And when this trusted confidant also left the land she continued to write him about her state of mind – but turned also with her songs of suffering and salvation to Thomas Wentworth Higginson.

8

In November of 1861, Samuel Bowles, editor of the *Springfield Republican* and intimate friend of Austin and Sue Dickinson, rented an apartment for his wife Mary and himself at the Brevoort House in New York City. Mary Bowles had experienced several stillbirths and, with a new baby soon to be born, had come to New York for special care; Bowles, severely afflicted with sciatica, would also be undergoing treatment. 'Dr. Barker has been in to see us several times', wrote Bowles to a friend, 'and has got us both under his care – promising to bring us both out right'.[32] In late December he wrote to another friend of the safe arrival of 'Young master Charles Allen' ('I wonder if ever baby was born, the object of more anxiety beforehand and felicitation afterward').[33]

Emily Dickinson had come to know Samuel and Mary Bowles when they became an intimate part of the Austin Dickinson circle in 1858; during his frequent visits to the Evergreens, the Springfield editor (sometimes accompanied by his wife, more often not) would also stop in at the Homestead. Samuel Bowles became an especially valued friend during Emily Dickinson's period of crisis; in October of 1861, a month after the terror she could tell to none, she wrote to convey sympathy to Bowles, undergoing a water-cure for his sciatica in nearby Northampton – and she also apologised for not seeing him during one of his visits (' . . . something troubled me – and I knew you needed light – and air – so I did'nt come' [L241]). Shortly after the arrival of the new baby at the Brevoort House (announced in the *Springfield Republican* on 20 December), she wrote to tell Mary Bowles 'how glad I am – and how glad we all are' about the new baby ('Tell him – I've got a pussy – for him – with a spotted Gown – and a Dog – with Ringlets – ' [L244]). Three weeks later, about 11 January, she wrote again to the Brevoort House – this time to Samuel Bowles. The opening sentences of her letter suggest that she is enclosing a poem intended, perhaps – Thomas Johnson suggests – 'to reveal something of a personal nature':[34] 'Are you willing?' she asks her friend; 'I am so far from Land – To offer *you* the cup – it might some Sabbath come *my* turn – Of wine how solemn – full!' The remainder of this brief letter conveys the hope that he will soon return and the good wishes of her family for his recovery ('When you tire with pain – to know that eyes would cloud, in Amherst – might that comfort – some?'). A postscript informs Bowles that 'We never forget Mary – ' (L247). This letter – and the letters and poems sent during the next months – establishes Bowles as a trusted and indispensable confidant. The substance and drift of the letters she sent to Samuel and Mary Bowles at the time of the misenveloping episode with Reverend Dwight – precisely fixed in mid-December of 1861 and early January of 1862—also definitively rules out Bowles as 'the friend who loves me – and thinks me larger than I am – ' and as Emily Dickinson's beloved 'Master'; the letters and poems sent to Bowles after he too left the land clearly establish him as a beloved confidant – one who was entrusted not with her love but with the secret of her love and sacred vocation.

Samuel Bowles, the man Emily Dickinson chose to confide in, was an indefatigable journalist and traveller – a witty and independent thinker and writer with a passion for life and a gift for deep and enduring friendships. On his visits to the Evergreens (and the Homestead) he brought a warmth and ebullience especially welcome in those austere households. Years after his death Emily Dickinson affectionately evoked his lively way with words and his pleasure in playfully bewildering his friends: 'You remember his swift way of wringing and flinging away a Theme, and others picking it up and gazing bewildered after him, and the prance that crossed his Eye at such times was unrepeatable – ' (L908).[35] And, on seeing a notice of the forthcoming biography of Bowles, she wrote to Bowles's dearest friend, Maria Whitney, to recall another example of his humour: 'On his last arriving from California he told us the Highwayman did not say your money or your life, but have you read Daniel Deronda – ' (L974).[36] And there was also a religious feeling in the journalist – a feeling free of cant and conventionality – that must have appealed to the poet; after first experiencing the grandeur of Yosemite, Bowles wrote: 'It was the confronting of God face to face, as in great danger, in solemn sudden death. All that was mortal shrank back, all that was immortal swept to the front and bent down in awe.'[37] In the same letter in which she recalled the episode about Bowles and *Daniel Deronda* to Maria Whitney, Emily Dickinson also mentioned how 'fitting' it was that Merriam's new biography of Bowles and Cross's *Life* of George Eliot should be appearing almost simultaneously. Bowles's enthusiasm for the English novelist was shared by Dickinson. George Eliot's open defiance of Victorian convention in her 'marriage' to G. H. Lewes (a married man unable to divorce his wife) was a subject of perennial interest to Emily Dickinson; it had a direct bearing on her interest in the intense and longstanding relationship between Maria Whitney and Samuel Bowles – a relationship that began early in 1861 (if not earlier), that for a time threatened his marriage, that did not end until his death.[38] Emily Dickinson's numerous letters to Miss Whitney – written during Bowles's final illness and over many years after his death – display sympathy and tact, and a deep understanding of her suffering ('I have thought of you often since the darkness', she wrote when he died, ' – though we cannot assist another's night' [L537]). Several months after Bowles's death, the poet wrote about a visit from Helen Hunt Jackson and her husband 'who told me that love of Mr Bowles and longing for some trace of him, led them to his house [in Springfield], and to seek his wife'. Reports about Mary Bowles's difficult and jealous temperament were widely known – but the Jacksons found the widow 'a stricken woman, though not so ruthless as they feared'. Concerning further links to her dead husband, Mary Bowles 'spoke with peculiar love of Miss Whitney of Northampton, and almost thought of accompanying them as far as yourself'. The poet reports these facts honoring Bowles and the woman he loved; and she closes her letter with sentences conveying an understanding of the great price Maria Whitney had paid for that love – and of the greatness and permanence of that love:

> To know that long fidelity in ungracious soil was not wholly squandered, might be sweet to you.
> I hope that you are well, and in full receipt of the Great Spirit whose leaving life was leaving you. (L573)

In the first of the series of letters seeking out Bowles as confidant and entrusting him with her secret – the one sent to the Brevoort House in January 1862 (L247) – Emily Dickinson shows an awareness of his relationship with Maria Whitney (who had spent a great deal of time with him while he was taking the water-cure in Northampton the previous fall) in her offer to perform a similar confiding service for him. She addresses him – in another letter – as a dear friend who will understand her state (Queen of Calvary) because he too is a lover-sufferer, one of the 'people of "Chillon"' (a prisoner forcibly separated from his beloved): 'If I amaze[d] your kindness – My Love is my only apology. To the people of "Chillon" – this – is enoug[h] I have met – no othe[rs.] Would you – ask le[ss] for your *Queen* – M[r] Bowles?' Her indebtedness to him, she observes, transcends any expression of gratitude ('To *"thank"* you – [s]hames my thought!').

The fact that her 'Love' is her apology is a reference to *her* beloved; she closes her letter with a poem that makes clear her deep feeling for her friend and understanding of his plight as a fellow-sufferer:

> [Sh]ould you but fail [at] – Sea –
> [In] sight of me –
> [Or] doomed lie –
> [Ne]xt Sun – to die –
> [O]r rap – at Paradise – unheard
> I'd *harass God*
> Until he let [you] in!
>
> (L249)

On another occasion, she responded to what may have been a questioning by Bowles about the depth of her suffering with another poem that may have included her valued friend and herself in the 'stately – shriven – Company – ' whose faith is 'the everlasting troth – ':

If you doubted my Snow – for a moment – you never will – again – I know –

Because I could not say it – I fixed it in the Verse – for you to read – when your thought wavers, for such a foot as mine –

> Through the strait pass of suffering –
> The Martyrs – even trod.
> Their feet – upon Temptation –
> Their faces – upon God –
>
> A stately – shriven – Company –
> Convulsion – playing round –
> Harmless – as streaks of Meteor –
> Upon a Planet's Bond –
>
> Their faith – the everlasting troth –
> Their Expectation – fair –
> The Needle – to the North Degree –
> Wades – so – thro' polar Air!
>
> (L251)

Emily Dickinson here draws on – and transforms – a James Montgomery hymn about martyrs, 'What are these in bright array', for her own hymn on another gathering of sufferers.[39]

Dandurand has suggested that Dickinson's poem may have been a response to an article reprinted in Bowles's *Republican*, 'Our Martyrs and Their Resurrection', on writers who achieve recognition only after their deaths. Dandurand sees in this and in similar letters and enclosed poems addressed to Bowles – including the extraordinary 'Title divine is mine!' – announcements to a valued friend and editor that will discourage his printing of her poems and remind him of her status as a poet dedicated to a calling that must avoid the public eye, that can flourish only in privacy.[40] I would urge further that Dickinson's dedicated calling is integrally linked to her mystical marriage: 'I wish that I were great, like Mr – Michael Angelo, and could paint for you', she wrote in 1858 to the Master to whom her sacred vocation was dedicated (ML, 15).

She had found in Bowles – during the terrible months of crisis in late 1861 and early 1862—a kindred believer in an 'everlasting troth' not to be realized on earth; by reaching out to him, by sharing her secret suffering with him, she was strengthened to bear her own burden. Even before turning to Bowles, she had been fixing 'in Verse' scores of poems to convey the ecstasy and anguish she 'could not say'. In April of 1862, Bowles followed the urgings of friends and his business partner and departed for Europe for an extended vacation designed to restore his precarious health; and in April of 1862, Emily Dickinson initiated a correspondence with Thomas Wentworth Higginson – who provided literary counsel and friendly encouragement and who (she informed him on two occasions) 'saved my Life'. She readily assented to Higginson's advice that she not publish ('that being foreign to my thought, as Firmament to Fin' [L265]). She was finding ways to ascend, through 'Calvaries of Love', to a state of grace true to herself and to the God of her inmost need. In the James Montgomery hymn, on which she drew for her own poem on martyr-sufferers, the martyrs are 'Clad in raiment pure and white'. She had come to her Master 'in white' – and now she wore only white and did not 'cross my Father's ground to any House or Town' (she later informed Higginson). When Bowles came to her house after his return from Europe in November of 1862, she sent word down that she could not see him. And she wrote, in a note of explanation: 'Forgive me if I prize the Grace – superior to the Sign' (L277). She had found her vocation as a maker of hymns and would follow it. The words of Isaac Watts, a maker of hymns in an earlier age, now applied with even greater force to Emily Dickinson: 'My tongue broke out in unknown strains, / and sung surprising grace.'[41]

9

The correspondence between Emily Dickinson and Charles Wadsworth seems to have been an extensive one, but their letters – except for the 'Master' letter-drafts possibly directed to him, and one undated letter from Wadsworth to Dickinson – have not survived. But sprinkled among Dickinson's numerous letters to her longstanding close friends, Dr and Mrs J. G. Holland, are evidences of the fact that they served as intermediaries for her communications to the minister. (Dr Holland was an editor and part-owner of the *Springfield Republican*; the Hollands were the Springfield hosts of the Dickinson sisters at least twice during the early 1850s.) 'I ask you [she wrote to Elizabeth Holland in October 1879] to ask your Doctor will he be so kind as to write the name of my Philadelphia friend on the Note within and your little Hand will take it to him – ' (L619; see also L475, L525, L547, L687). (A next-door neighbor, Luke Sweetser, is reported to have transmitted Wadsworth's letters to her.)[42]

In 1869, Wadsworth left Calvary Church and San Francisco to return to his beloved Philadelphia, where he served as pastor of several congregations before his sudden death on the first of April 1882. In the funeral address, the Reverend John DeWitt observed that Wadsworth's service as pastor at the Arch Street Church from 1850 to 1862 'was probably the period of his widest popularity and his greatest power'. His pastorate at the Calvary Church was also highly successful – but, on his return to Philadelphia, there was a pronounced drop in his popularity not, DeWitt observes, because of any loss of intellectual power (his last sermons had all the force and power of those delivered in his best days) but because of 'a diminution of the power of the organs of speech'.[43]

DeWitt's funeral tribute went beyond the usual expressions of sorrow for the loss of this dedicated and eloquent servant of God to emphasize a temperament and way of life that set Wadsworth far apart from the lives of others. Though highly honored and widely known as a minister, DeWitt says in his opening sentence, Wadsworth led a personal life so secluded 'that few of his own congregation and few of his professional brethren knew him well or saw him often, elsewhere than in the pulpit'. He was not lacking in affection for his fellow ministers, but his temperament was such that he could not, 'without painful and exhausting physical effort', converse and exchange ideas with them; DeWitt compared this unusual and powerful minister to John Chrysostom who would come from the seclusion of his cell in Antioch to the pulpit of the cathedral and, after delivering his discourse, 'disappear as if he were a messenger from another world'.[44] Wadsworth's secluded life, he further observed, was not wholly a misfortune: His sermons might have otherwise lacked the concentration and lofty power that they possessed ('He spoke out like a Hebrew prophet whom his lofty theme was enough to satisfy, and to whom it was unknown whether men heard or did not hear'). DeWitt offered, finally, comfort in this hour of great loss – comfort in the message Wadsworth himself would offer could he speak today: He would bid us, 'in the pain of our earthly pilgrimage, think of the glory that is sure to be its outcome'. And he would tell us of the heaven that awaits us: 'Canaan lies bright and fair before us; and this path that lies through the desert is the only path that leads to its enrapturing inheritance.'

The Reverend DeWitt does not, in his funeral address, refer to the stormy circumstances that preceded and accompanied Wadsworth's move from Philadelphia to San Francisco two decades earlier. (According to DeWitt, Wadsworth 'felt compelled, for reasons connected with his health', to accept the call from Calvary Church.)[45] But some intimation of that stormy Civil War period in the history of the nation and the church may linger in the martial imagery of one of the series of resolutions adopted and transmitted to Wadsworth's bereaved family by Calvary Church, San Francisco:

> *Resolved*, 4th. That while he was strictly Calvinistic and Presbyterian in all his teachings he was free from all taint of sectarianism, rejoicing at all times to say a hearty "God-speed" to every soldier of the cross, whatever the uniform he wore, and whatever the colors he marched under.[46]

In her third letter to Master ('If you saw a bullet'), Emily Dickinson tells of a wish she cannot repress 'that mine were the Queen's place – ' (ML, 35–6); the following resolution adopted by Calvary Church employs royal imagery to pay tribute to the dead minister – imagery that, though somewhat conventional, parallels Dickinson's tribute to her royal 'Master' (to whom it was forbidden her 'To come nearer than Presbyteries – '):

> *Resolved*, 5th. That he was a man of one idea – the pulpit his throne, and he knowing it, endeavoring at all time to fill it with kingly presence.[47]

10

After his death, Emily Dickinson conveyed her deep feelings about
Charles Wadsworth to Elizabeth Holland: 'All other Surprise is at
last monotonous, but the Death of the Loved is all moments – *now* –
Love has but one Date – "The first of April" "Today, Yesterday and
Forever" – ' (L801). To her beloved Judge Lord, she wrote:

> I am told it is only a pair of Sundays since you went from me. I
> feel it many years. Today [30 April 1882] is April's last – It has
> been an April of meaning to me. I have been in your Bosom.
> My Philadelphia has passed from Earth, and the Ralph Waldo
> Emerson – whose name my Father's Law Student taught me, has
> touched the secret Spring. Which Earth are we in? (L750)

'My Philadelphia' was the poet's designation for Wadsworth; Lord
was a native of Salem and she called him, on occasion, 'my lovely
Salem'.

In August 1882, James D. Clark wrote to Emily Dickinson –
and enclosed a volume of the dead minister's sermons. He was
Wadsworth's closest friend and the correspondence released in the
poet some deep, and deeply guarded, emotions. During the next
four years – right up to the last month of her life – she exchanged
numerous revealing letters with the Clark brothers centering on
Wadsworth ('the third Member of the sundered Trio', she called
him after the death of James Clark [L880]). She shared with the
Clarks the news of bereavements: the death of her mother, of her
nephew Gilbert, of Judge Lord. But Wadsworth was the inexhaust-
ible subject for restless inquiry and deeply felt reminiscence.

In her last letter to Charles Clark – written a month before her
death – she expresses gratitude for every detail he has related
and can yet relate about Wadsworth ('Thank you for each circumstance, and tell me all you love to say of what said your lost
Brother "The Doctor opened his Heart to Charlie"' [L1040]). What
confidences had Wadsworth transmitted to Charles Clark? None
of the Clarks' letters has survived but it is possible to reconstruct
some details about Wadsworth's 'Life of Ambush' from Emily
Dickinson's twenty-one letters written to answer them. The Clarks
must have known about Wadsworth's deep feeling for the poet;
James Clark's first letter to her (enclosing some of Wadsworth's
sermons) may well have been sent at the dying minister's request.

In her reply, Dickinson asks if Wadsworth's children 'were near him at last, or if they grieved to lose that most sacred life' (L773). Her third letter responds to new information that James Clark has conveyed ('The Griefs of which you speak were unknown to me') and conveys her own sense of Wadsworth's troubled life 'full of dark secrets' – as the minister himself had on one occasion described it (L776). The griefs described by James Clark are very likely those referred to by the poet in one of her last letters to Charles Clark: '... and did his Daughter regret her flight from her loved Father, or the son who left the Religion so precious to him?' (L1039). The daughter in flight from her father (Edith, born in 1858), and the son in rebellion against his father's religion (Charles, Jr, born in 1860) point to domestic tensions known to Wadsworth's closest friends, the Clarks – tensions which Emily Dickinson must have sensed long before James Clark confided in her about their dead friend's private trouble. Indeed, her inquiry about the minister's children at the time of his death – whether they were with him at the last, whether they felt grief at his death – suggests that she may have known more about Wadsworth's estrangement from these children than she admits to knowing.

According to Emily Dickinson (in her third letter to James Clark), Wadsworth was reticent about himself and 'never spoke of his home, but of a Child – "Willie," whom, forgive me the arrogance, he told me was like me ... ' (L776). (The reference to 'Willie' [William Scott Wadsworth, born in 1868] may have been incorporated into one of Wadsworth's letters during the 1870s – or it may have been made during his last visit, in 1880.) In this same letter, she thanks Clark for the photograph of Wadsworth he had sent – and for the warning, however unnecessary, that she hold in confidence the information he has provided concerning the minister's private troubles ('thank you for the Face ... and for the monition, tho' to disclose a grief of his I could not surmise – '). It is noteworthy that Clark should initiate the correspondence by sending Wadsworth's sermons, that he should send, without being requested to do so, Wadsworth's photograph – and that he should confide in her about the minister's private troubles. 'I have lost since writing you [she informed Charles Clark shortly after Judge Lord's death], another cherished friend, a word of whom I enclose – and how to repair my shattered ranks is a besetting pain' (L896). She had shared with Lord her grief over the death of Wadsworth; now she was sharing, however guardedly (her lover must be no more than 'another cherished friend'), her grief over Judge Lord with Wadsworth's most intimate friend. Her references to Wadsworth are generally elegiac and restrained – but a more intimate and playful note is occasionally sounded.

In her first letter to James Clark, she tells of the minister's last visit to her house (two years before his death) – of his unexpected arrival and their opening exchange:

> He rang one summer evening to my glad surprise – "Why did you not tell me you were coming, so I could have it to hope for," I said – "Because I did not know it myself. I stepped from my Pulpit to the Train," was his quiet reply. (L766)

She repeats this account four years later in her last letter to Charles Clark; some of the language and details are slightly different – but it is essentially the same account; and both versions have the ring of loving and faithful recollection:

> The last time he came in Life, I was with my Lilies and Heliotropes, said my sister to me, "the Gentleman with the deep voice wants to see you, Emily," hearing him ask of the servant. "Where did you come from," I said, for he spoke like an Apparition.
>
> "I stepped from my Pulpit to the Train" was [his] simple reply, and when I asked "how long," "Twenty Years" said he with inscrutable roguery – . . . (L1040)

To the Clarks, early and late, the poet presents a striking vignette of a powerful man of God wryly aware of the impulsiveness that brought him, suddenly, to Amherst: He has moved from pulpit to train without prior notice because 'I did not know it myself'. His reply to her question is a quiet one; he is 'the Gentleman with the deep voice' who speaks 'like an Apparition'. Both accounts – though separated by four years – reveal something important about Wadsworth and the Wadsworth–Dickinson relationship. That he was important to her is clear; equally clear is her great attraction for him. His impulsiveness in coming to her so precipitously from Philadelphia – and in informing her of the fact – points to a deep involvement and understanding on both sides. The 'inscrutable roguery' displayed by the minister when he referred to the twenty years that had somehow elapsed between visits demonstrated a playfulness the poet understood and practiced in her own discourse.

Wadsworth's enormous importance to Emily Dickinson – to the end of her life – may be gauged by a startling statement that she made to Charles Clark in early January of 1884. Twenty years earlier, in March of 1863, Samuel Bowles was already describing her as 'the Queen Recluse'; Mabel Todd wrote of the reports she had heard about Emily Dickinson shortly after moving to Amherst in 1881: 'For nearly twenty years she had not left the house and grounds, for the last ten years the house was her only abode . . . . ' The poet rarely saw any person other than family members and the family servants; when Mabel Todd came to play the piano and sing for her, she listened from an invisible perch on the staircase – and sent in some wine and cake (and a poem) to thank the performer.[48] Among the few persons she accepted as visitors were Wadsworth, Thomas Wentworth Higginson ('I never was with any one who drained my nerve power so much', he informed his wife [L342b]), and Lord. It was, therefore, extraordinary for Emily Dickinson to ask Charles Clark to come to see her – to share memories with her about Wadsworth:

> You seem by some deep Accident, to be the only tie between the Heaven that evanesced, and the Heaven that stays.
>   I hope the winged Days that bear you to your Brother are not too destitute of Song, and wish that we might speak with you of him and of yourself, and of the third Member of that sundered Trio. Perhaps another spring would call you to Northampton, and Memory might invite you here. (L880)

Her rare gesture was prompted by Clark's 'sacred kindness' in response to an earlier letter written soon after the sudden death of her beloved nephew Gilbert; without mentioning her latest bereavement, a crushing blow, she referred to disquieting thoughts – distilled into a great meditation on flesh and spirit, life and death, that she encloses:

> The Spirit lasts – but in what mode –
> Below, the Body speaks,
> But as the Spirit furnishes –
> Apart, it never talks –
> The Music in the Violin
> Does not emerge alone
> But Arm in Arm with Touch, yet Touch

> Alone – is not a Tune –
> The Spirit lurks within the Flesh
> Like Tides within the Sea
> That make the Water live, estranged
> What would the Either be?

The interdependence of flesh and spirit are incisively evoked by tropes that link the vitality of music and the sea to touch and tide: The violin requires touch to come alive; the sea is animated by the tides. In the closing lines of the poem, Dickinson's persona poses the crucial question: Will the fusion of flesh and spirit transcend death and time?

> Does that know – now – or does it cease –
> That which to this is done,
> Resuming at a mutual date
> With every future one?
> Instinct pursues the Adamant,
> Exacting this Reply –
> Adversity if it may be, or
> Wild Prosperity,
> The Rumor's Gate was shut so tight
> Before my Mind was sown,
> Not even a Prognostic's Push
> Could make a Dent thereon –
>
> (L872)[49]

Dickinson's lexicon helps to clarify a key line in the passage just quoted ('Instinct pursues the Adamant'): There *instinct* is defined as 'the exercise of certain natural powers directed to the present or future good of the individual'; and Chaucer is cited for his use of *adamant* (in *Romance of the Rose*) as 'the lodestone'. In 'The Spirit lasts – ' instinct reaches out (blindly and truly) to the unreachable lodestone, a knowledge of eternity. Rumor's gate is shut tight and the outcome is uncertain. But the lodestone keeps exerting its pull.

The Reverend Gladden had assured her that immortality was true – though 'Absolute demonstration there can be none of this truth' (L752a). Wadsworth is gone from the earth – and she prefaces the poem she copied out for Charles Clark ('The Spirit lasts – but in what mode – ') with a reference to the dead minister: 'These thoughts disquiet me, and the great friend is gone who could solace them. Do they disturb you?'(L872). Wadsworth's vision of heaven (discussed in Chapter 4, below) was both a solace and goad to Emily Dickinson. Her grief over the death of little Gilbert intensified her need for her 'dearest earthly friend' – and she was moved, in her next letter, to invite his closest friend.)

11

The extraordinary portrait of Charles Wadsworth that emerges from Emily Dickinson's four-year correspondence with the Clark brothers bears a striking resemblance to the way the minister is described by the Reverend George Burrowes (during Wadsworth's pastorate at Calvary Church) – and by the Reverend DeWitt (in his funeral address). Burrowes tells how all who hear Wadsworth must 'feel that behind all he says there must be lying years of sorrow and agony' – and how this eloquent preacher 'shrinks from public notoriety, public demonstrations, and public applause'. Wadsworth seems to have little awareness of his own magnetic appeal and finds it difficult, in his humility, to mingle with the throngs who have been deeply moved by him. Reverend DeWitt, in his funeral address, sees Wadsworth's secluded life as a source of his power; as mentioned earlier, he is compared to the saintly John Chrysostom who would deliver his sermon and disappear as if from another world.[50]

For Emily Dickinson the life and powerful message of Charles Wadsworth was that of the suffering Christ. She knew him 'a Man of sorrow', she wrote to James Clark early in their correspondence – 'a Dusk Gem, born of troubled Waters, astray in any Crest below'. Dickinson frequently dwelled on the redemptive suffering of Christ as an enlarging and sanctifying force in the lives of those she loved – and in herself; but she had little to say about the resurrected Christ – and poked fun at orthodox visions of a general resurrection in several poems (discussed in Chapter Four, below). The poem she incorporated into her letter to Clark is, therefore, especially noteworthy for it commemorates Wadsworth by linking the dead minister to the risen Christ:

> Obtaining but his own extent
> In whatsoever Realm –
> 'Twas Christ's own personal Expanse
> That bore him from the Tomb.

The possibility that this 'Dusk Gem' has reached beyond mortal limits to an unknown realm is enlarged by Christ's suffering as a living person – by his 'own personal Expanse'.[51]

Christ's example offers consolation to those who mourn Wadsworth – and she speculates, at the close of her letter to Clark, about the possibility of a reunion in some other realm: 'I do not yet fathom that he has died – and hope I may not till he assist me in another World – "Hallowed be it's Name"!'(L776) Dickinson here translates the prayer offered to the people by Jesus, in Matthew 6:9 ('Our Father which art in heaven, Hallowed be thy name'), to a prayer that makes hallowed the site of a reunion, should it take place, between the minister and the poet. This is the kind of heresy that set Emily Dickinson far apart from Christian orthodoxy – but not from the wide-ranging sympathies of Charles Wadsworth.

2

Sacred Texts Transformed

Emily Dickinson read voraciously all of her life: Among the writers of her own century, she had an intimate acquaintanceship with Keats, Byron, Wordsworth, the Brownings, the Brontë sisters, Dickens, George Eliot, Hawthorne, Emerson, Longfellow, Tennyson, Ruskin – and others. But her most passionate involvement was with the sacred texts of the Renaissance and eighteenth century: Shakespeare; the King James Version of the Bible; Isaac Watts's vast outpouring of hymns; the devotional prose of Thomas à Kempis and Sir Thomas Browne; the devotional poetry of George Herbert and Henry Vaughan. This passionate involvement was accompanied by an equally intense determination, in her own writings, not to borrow from those she read and admired. 'I marked a line in One Verse – [she informed Higginson] because I met it after I made it – and never consciously touch a paint, mixed by another person' (L271). Instead, Shakespeare, the King James Bible, Watts, and some notable seventeenth-century writers of devotional prose and poetry served as catalysts to release Dickinson's distinctive voice and vision – a voice and vision that transformed these sacred texts to serve her own religious quest and dedicated artistry.

1

Shakespeare was rarely far from Emily Dickinson's consciousness from girlhood to the end of her life. On several occasions, she summed up her feelings about him in language vividly recorded by Higginson in 1870: 'After long disuse of her eyes [she was treated for eye trouble in 1864] she read Shakespeare & thought why is any other book needed' (L342b).[1] To others, she reported with equal fervor that 'he has had his Future who has found Shakespeare' (L402); and that 'to have been suspected of writing

35

[Shakespeare's works], was the most beautiful stigma of Bacon's Life – ' (L721). But Dickinson's intense admiration was accompanied by an awareness of the way Shakespeare's stormy pageantry and profound knowledge pale in the light of the drama of ordinary human existence:

> Drama's Vitallest Expression is the Common Day
> That arise and set about Us –
> Other Tragedy
>
> Perish in the Recitation –
> This – the best enact
> When the Audience is scattered
> and the Boxes shut –
>
> "Hamlet" to Himself were Hamlet –
> Had not Shakespeare wrote –
> Though the "Romeo" left no Record
> Of his Juliet,
>
> It were infinite enacted
> In the Human Heart
> Only Theatre recorded
> Owner cannot shut –
>
> (741, about 1863)

Dickinson's persona marches us (in hymn book metre) past vacant theatre, past the imperishable characters of the imperishable Bard – to that which is 'infinite enacted / In the Human Heart – ' It is Hamlet (as the maker of this poem well knew) who counsels the players against exaggeration and false expression, who reminds them that the whole purpose of their art 'was and is, to hold, as 'twere, the mirror up to nature' (III.i.16–22); and it is Hamlet who understands the power of a play to effect through art what would otherwise be an impossible task: ' – the play's the thing / Wherein I'll catch the conscience of the king' (II.ii.604-5). Dickinson also knew well the many eloquent passages in other plays in which the distinction between the real world and the world of the theatre is magically dissolved. Shakespeare's greatness is to convey with irresistible power, through his insight into both worlds (and through artful mirrorings), the truth spoken by the banished duke in *As You Like It*: 'This wide and universal theatre / Presents more woeful pageants than the scene / Wherein we play' (II.vii.137–9). The six words that conclude her poem ('Only Theatre recorded / Owner cannot shut – ') are Dickinson's laconic and masterful rendering of that truth.

Dickinson's thorough familiarity included the English history plays – and such early works as *1 Henry VI* ('I read a few words since I came home – ' she wrote to her cousin early in 1865, 'John Talbot's parting with his son, and Margaret's with Suffolk. I read them in the garret, and the rafters wept' [L304]). The striking expression she used in what seems the first letter she wrote to Samuel Bowles taking him into her closest confidence – appended to the poem 'Title divine – is mine!' – is her variation on a refrain frequently sounded in Shakespeare, most notably in *Richard II*: 'Honor is it's own pawn', she wrote to Bowles (and again in her first letter to Higginson a short time later); in Shakespeare's play, on three occasions, characters are challenged with some visible sign of 'honour's pawn' (by Bolingbroke, I.i.74; by an unnamed Lord, IV.i.55; and by Surrey, IV.i.70).[2] But Shakespeare's 'tragedy of the King's Two Bodies', as Ernst H. Kantorowicz describes *Richard II*,[3] provided more than a significant phrase to Emily Dickinson during her time of greatest crisis. Kantorowicz is referring to 'the godhead and manhood of a king,' a central concept in Shakespeare's play: 'The breath of worldly men', says King Richard in the course of his struggle, 'cannot depose / The deputy elected by the Lord' (III.ii.56–7). It is Richard himself who, eventually, 'With mine own hands' deposes himself and 'With mine own breath' releases his subjects from their 'duteous oaths' (IV.i.203ff). In this ultimate act of self-sacrifice, Richard sees himself as a direct counterpart of Christ – his enemies 'Pilates / [who] Have here delivered me to my sour cross' (IV.i.240–1). It seems clear that Dickinson drew repeatedly on Shakespeare's conception of sacred royalty to represent in her poems a lover's – and her own – sacred suffering and transcendent triumph.

In her third letter to her Master ('If you saw a bullet'), she had offered as her only apology for her overpowering wish 'that mine were the Queen's place' her 'love of the – Plantagenet' (ML, 36) – an evocation of royalty that links her beloved and embattled Master to the embattled King Richard. Richard's special significance to Dickinson may have been that he was, in the words of E. M. W. Tillyard, 'authentic heir of the crusading Plantagenets' – one who 'had the full sanction of the medieval kingship and the strong pathos of being the last king to possess it'.[4] Emily Dickinson's expression of the irrepressible wish for 'the Queen's place' and her 'love of the – Plantagenet' is immediately followed by the complaint that she is forbidden 'To come nearer than Presbyteries' – and to approach her Master as lover (' – the prank of the Heart at play on the Heart – in holy Holiday – is forbidden me – '). This reference to 'Presbyteries' coupled with her fear, conveyed in the same letter, that he might forget her 'in fight, or flight – or the foreign land' seem to provide glimpses of Wadsworth's embattled position, in 1861, that make her metaphorical flights more graspable and understandable. In a very real sense, Wadsworth's governing presbyteries sent him into exile to 'the foreign land' – and in a very real sense it was a self-imposed exile.

2

The imagery of sacred royalty in Shakespeare and in the Bible converge in numerous poems that announce her new royal station, the Christlike suffering and triumph of her beloved and herself, her dedication to her sacred vocation. In his history plays, Shakespeare drew heavily on medieval traditions involving the close relationship between Church and State: the Church was the mystical body of Christ (Christ the head and the 'totality of Christian society' its members); the State was 'directed by the king as the vicar of Christ and guided by the ministers of the Church . . . . ' – and the people 'not simply the sum of individuals of a community but "men assembled into one mystical body"'.[5] Underlying these conceptions of Church and State polity is Paul's metaphor: 'For as the body is one, and hath many members, and all the members of that one body, being many, are one body: also is Christ' (1 Corinthians 12:12).

To all these concepts and concerns as reflected in the Bible and in her beloved Shakespeare was Emily Dickinson responsive in 'He put the Belt around my life – ' (273),[6] one of a series of poems written to announce and celebrate the new relationship she has entered into with her imperial Master. In the incisive measure of Watts, her opening stanza (there are two eight-line double-stanzas in Common Metre) compresses Shakespeare's stormy pageantry into an intense picture of a personal investiture bringing with it a new fealty and sacred dedication:

He put the Belt around my life –

> I heard the Buckle snap –
> And turned away, imperial,
> My Lifetime folding up –
> Deliberate, as a Duke would do
> A Kingdom's Title Deed –
> Henceforth, a Dedicated sort –
> A Member of the Cloud.

Her imperial Master has invested Dickinson's persona with a new rank; his ceremonial act is likened to a prince's acquisition and disposition of 'A Kingdom's Title Deed – ' Transformed, she is now 'a Dedicated sort – / A member of the Cloud.' Higginson expressed puzzlement to Mrs Todd about this last phrase during their preparation of *Poems*, Second Series (1891); 'is it "a member of the cloud"', he asked, '& what does it mean? "A member of the breed" would be intelligible & rhyme.' Mrs Todd replied that the manuscript did indeed read '"A member of the cloud," in the original, and I suppose simply means to express the great loftiness by the love given, which made her "fold up" her liftetime, "henceforth a dedicated sort."'[7] To further explicate Emily Dickinson's baffling phrase, Mrs Todd could have directed Higginson, a former minister, to Holy Scripture. Among the numerous references there, two are representative: 'Moreover, brethren', says Paul, 'I would not that ye should be ignorant, how that all our fathers were . . . baptized unto Moses in the cloud and in the sea' (1 Corinthians 10:1–2); and in Revelation the resurrected dead 'ascended up to heaven in a cloud' (11:12).

The second, and concluding, stanza of 'He put the Belt around my life' defines the future mode of existence of one whose fealty has been secured and is now 'a member of the cloud':

> Yet not too far to come at call –
> And do the little Toils
> That make the Circuit of the Rest –
> And deal occasional smiles
> To lives that stoop to notice mine –
> And kindly ask it in –
> Whose invitation, know you not
> For Whom I must decline?

She must live her daily life of routine obligation and social courtesy – up to a point. He who put the belt around her life has put her under sacred obligation; she must not, cannot, accept the invitation of others to enter other lives.[8]

There are many instances in both the Bible and Shakespeare of miraculous change effected by God's (or His Son's) touch – and that of earthly, i.e., royal, representatives. One of Emily Dickinson's most moving love poems, written in about 1862, tells of such a touch – and of the transfiguration that followed:

> He touched me, so I live to know
> That such a day, permitted so,
> I groped upon his breast –
> It was a boundless place to me
> And silenced, as the awful sea
> Puts minor streams to rest.
>
> And now, I'm different from before,
> As if I breathed superior air –
> Or brushed a Royal Gown –
> My feet, too, that had wandered so –
> My Gypsy face – transfigured now –
> To tenderer Renown –
>
> Into this Port, if I might come,
> Rebecca, to Jerusalem,
> Would not so ravished turn –
> Nor Persian, baffled at her shrine
> Lift such a Crucifixal sign
> To her imperial Sun.
>
> (506)[9]

His touch allowed Dickinson's persona to find a resting place 'Upon his breast' as 'boundless' as the sea – and as pacifying as a great sea absorbing its turbulent tributaries. Her royal transfiguration has ended all restless wandering and if she could know her place in his heart were secure she would turn as eagerly to him as Rebecca to her spiritual homeland in Jerusalem. Cyrus, King of Persia, was moved by the word of the Lord to build 'the house of the Lord God of Israel . . . in Jerusalem' (2 Chronicles 36:23; Ezra 1:1–3); neither Rebecca, if she had lived to see it, nor Persian, baffled at the shrine built for Rebecca's people, would convey the reverential awe she waits to reveal to 'her imperial Sun'. (The sun symbolises both kingship and God; see, among many examples, *Richard II* [11.iv.22] and Psalms 84:11.) The sign that the transfigured lover displays to her beloved is 'Crucifixal' in part because he is a man of God suffering for his sacred commitments and convictions – in part because she worships him as he worships Christ. She is privileged to share his suffering; it is as inevitable a dimension of her worship as it is of his.

During this time of crisis, poems of celebration alternate with expressions of concern about the displeasure of her beloved. The passionate fusion of devotion and indignation in 'Doubt Me! My Dim Companion' evokes – in three double stanzas in Watts's Common Metre – Imogen's plight (in both senses of the term) in *Cymbeline*; the predominant note is queenly independence:

> Doubt Me! My Dim Companion!
> Why, God, would be content
> With but a fraction of the Life –
> Poured thee, without a stint –
> The whole of me – forever –
> What more the Woman can,
> Say quick, that I may dower thee
> With last Delight I own!
>
> It cannot be my Spirit –
> For that was thine, before –
> I ceded all of Dust I knew –
> What Opulence the more
> Had I – a freckled Maiden,
> Whose farthest of Degree,
> Was – that she might –
> Some distant Heaven,
> Dwell timidly, with thee!
>
> Sift her, from Brow to Barefoot!
> Strain till your last Surmise –
> Drop, like a Tapestry, away,
> Before the Fire's Eyes –
> Winnow her finest fondness –
> But hallow just the snow
> Intact, in Everlasting flake –
> Oh, Caviler, for you!

(275)

Imogen is, of course, the daughter of an English king and not to be strictly identified with the 'freckled Maiden' in Dickinson's poem. But there also seems little doubt that the unstinting love and loyalty that Imogen holds for Posthumus – and the trial that her exiled husband subjects her to – are reflected in the eloquent outcry of Dickinson's persona. The concluding stanza draws on the imagery, circumstantial detail and language of Shakespeare's play. The final remaining doubt of her beloved (his 'last Surmise – ') must finally drop away 'like a Tapestry'; she asks her doubting lover to separate out her imprudent passion ('Winnow her finest fondness – ') from the sacred and permanent love she bears for him, a love that merits not doubt but respectful reverence ('But hallow just the snow / Intact, in Everlasting flake – '). Among the damning evidences of Imogen's infidelity offered by the treacherous Iachimo is a description of the 'tapestry of silk and silver' hanging in her bedchamber (II.iv.68–9); Posthumus cries out, after being deceived by Iachimo, that he had mistakenly believed his wife to be 'As chaste as unsunn'd snow' (II.v.130–1); Cymbeline, in the closing scene, urges Iachimo to speak out – or 'bitter torture shall / Winnow the truth from falsehood' (V.v.130–1); Posthumus, on discovering the truth, cries out – too late (he thinks) to bring her back: 'O Imogen! / My queen, my life, my wife!' (V.v.226–7)

'Oh – did I offend it – [Did'nt it want me to tell it the truth]' exclaims Emily Dickinson to her Master, 'Daisy – Daisy – offend it – who bends her smaller life to his . . . every day – ' In this second Master letter, dated by Franklin in the spring of 1861, Emily Dickinson sets down and then cancels a pointed comment on his inability to tolerate the truth – and dwells instead on her overwhelming love ('a love so big it scares her'), her courage ('Daisy – who never flinched thro' that awful parting – '), her eagerness to offer solace to him ('who would have sheltered him in her childish bosom') (ML, 22). Despite a striking difference in tone – the resounding indignation of 'Doubt Me! My Dim Companion!' is paralleled in the Master letter only by a subdued (and suppressed) reference to his unwillingness to face the truth – the poem might well be read as a counterpart of the letter. The 'freckled maiden' of the poem may well be a transformed but recognizable version of the woman asking her Master to forgive 'her odd – Backwoodsman [life] ways . . . . '(ML, 25) Such a view is supported by a handwriting analysis of the manuscript poem: It seems to have been written in early 1861, just about the same time as Dickinson's letter to her Master.[10]

The lively independence earlier exhibited toward a lover who doubts her love is even more forcefully displayed in a poem written the following year; in it, Dickinson's persona announces her independence from family and community; though she may never have experienced baptism it was enough a part of her village world for Dickinson to reenact it – along with a second baptism, this one a baptismal crowning experienced (unlike the first) in the full consciousness of adulthood and womanhood, in the full exercise of free choice:

> I'm ceded – I've stopped being Their's –
> The name They dropped upon my face
> With water, in the country church
> Is finished using, now,
> And They can put it with my Dolls,
> My childhood, and the string of spools,
> I've finished threading – too –
> Baptized, before, without the choice,
> But this time, consciously, of Grace –
> Unto supremest name –
> Called to my Full – The Crescent dropped –
> Existence's whole Arc, filled up,
> With one small Diadem.
>
> My second Rank – too small the first –
> Crowned – Crowing – on my Father's breast –
> A half unconscious Queen –
> But this time – Adequate – Erect,
> With Will to choose, or to reject,
> And I choose, just a Crown –
>
> (508)[11]

Baptism was, on Biblical authority, associated with royalty; Peter conveyed the efficacy of baptismal unction when he addressed those newly converted as 'a chosen generation, a royal priesthood' (1 Peter 2:9).[12] Archbishop Cranmer had presided over the baptism of the infant Princess Elizabeth and (as recounted in Shakespeare's *Henry VIII*) prophesied future greatness for her and England. Cranmer's prophecy – elaborated from Holinshed's account of the christening – was incorporated into the concluding scene of *Henry VIII*, a scene Emily Dickinson may have transformed for her own poetic account of two baptisms: a village version of her own christening (her middle name was Elizabeth and she was occasionally called by that name),[13] a baptismal-coronation of the full-grown woman 'With Will to choose, or to reject' – who chooses 'just a Crown – ' In his prophecy, Cranmer envisions for the princess a life of 'many days . . . , / And yet no day without a deed to crown it'. She must die, for so the saints must have her, a virgin ('A most unspotted lily shall she pass / To th' ground, and all the world shall mourn her' [V.v.61–2]). The crown chosen by the persona in Dickinson's poem provides her with supreme exaltation ('Called to my Full – . . . / Existence's whole Arc, filled up, / With one small Diadem'); she is 'ceded' – to God and to the man of God who is her royal partner. (In what seems a companion poem, the narrator announces, at the triumphant close, that she is 'Baptized – this day – a Bride – ' [473].)

Dickinson's letters and poems are sprinkled with echoes from Shakespeare – echoes translated into her own intense vision of 'the Common Day'. In a letter (and enclosed poem) sent to a young friend on the eve of his marriage, she evokes the 'Prince Question' (posed by Polonius about the genuineness of Hamlet's love for Ophelia) – and Polonius' advice to Laertes:

> To ask of each that gathered Life, Oh, where did it grow, is intuitive.
> That you have answered this Prince Question to your own delight, is joy to us all.
>
> > Lad of Athens, faithful be
> > To Thyself,
> > And Mystery –
> > All the rest is Perjury –
> >
> > > (L865)[14]

'By intuition, Mightiest Things / Assert themselves – and not by terms – ' Dickinson's persona announces (420); both to ask and to seek to answer the question of where love springs from, she tells her friend, 'is intuitive' – springs from the mystery of living and dying. In its definition of *mystery*, her lexicon quotes from 1 Corinthians 2:7: 'we speak the wisdom of God in a mystery.' Polonius advises his son, above all, 'to thine own self be true' – and sets spies upon him and upon Hamlet. Dickinson fully understood Shakespeare's understanding of a counterfeit person who eloquently advocates authentic selfhood. Dickinson's persona, in 'Lad of Athens', asks her friend to be true not only to himself but to 'Mystery' – to those

fleeting glimpses of the wisdom of God available only to those truly
true to themselves.

3

It was in the Bible, the book Dickinson knew best, that she found
the most provocative glimpses of the 'Mystery' which she tried all
of her life to penetrate. (There were nineteen Bibles in the Dickinson
household.)[15] To her friend Joseph Lyman (in a letter recalling a time
in the mid or late 1850s), she conveyed her sense of rediscovery and
renewal on returning to that mighty book:

> Some years after we saw each other last I fell to reading the Old
> and New Testament. I had known it as an arid book but looking
> I saw how infinitely wise & how merry it is.
>
> Anybody that knows grammar must admit the surpassing
> splendor & force of its speech, but the fathomless gulfs of mean-
> ing – those words which He spoke to those most necessary to him,
> hints about some celestial reunion – yearning for a oneness – has
> any one fathomed that sea?[16]

To many about her, the words of the Bible 'are very near & necessary'
– and she wishes they were more so for her, 'for I see them shedding
a serenity quite wonderful & blessed'. It may have been during these
years, when she was launching her career as a poet and reaching
out to the spiritual guidance of Charles Wadsworth, that she was
probing deeper into the words of the Bible – words that reside
in 'the fathomless gulfs of meaning', words that hint at celestial
reunion and serenity for those who are isolated and troubled.

In one of her most extraordinary lyrics, Dickinson's persona claims
to have found the words for all thoughts but one; she describes
her failure and impotence with a stunning metaphorical flight
– a parable on man's vain search for God, on man's ultimate
awareness of God's presence; a parable on the poet's vain search
for the word that will adequately convey that ultimate awareness:

> I found the words to every thought
> I ever had – but One –
> And that – defies me –
> As a Hand did try to chalk the Sun
>
> To Races – nurtured in the Dark –

How would your own – begin?
Can Blaze be shown in Cochineal –
Or Noon – in Mazarin?

(581)[17]

The speaker's hyperbolic claim fixes our attention on the one
thought that defies expression. What can it be? No hint is offered
– but the awesome difficulty of conveying that thought is presented
with stunning directness and concreteness. The hand trying to chalk
the sun is real; the speaker evokes, in her spare and elliptical image,
a schoolroom for the blind. The teacher is at a blackboard and has
a formidable task. The closing lines point up the difficulty (i.e.,
impossibility) of capturing sunshine in a picture made by man –
a difficulty enlarged to staggering proportions when we learn that
the result will be shown 'To Races – nurtured in the Dark – ' It is
in the defiant thought for which words cannot be found that the
godhead resides – the godhead Dickinson tried to embody in many
of her poems.

'Life is the finest secret', she wrote to Elizabeth Holland in 1870,
and added: 'So long as that remains, we must all whisper' (L354).
To express sympathy to the convalescing Mrs Higginson, she quoted
from one of the parables of Jesus she knew and loved: 'I am sorry
you need Health, but rejoice you do not Affection – That can be
growing while you rest, for the Heart is the "seed" of which we
read that "the Birds of Heaven lodge in its Branches"' (L481). (She
is quoting freely from Matthew's version of Jesus' parable likening
the kingdom of heaven to a mustard seed 'Which indeed is the least
of all seeds: but when it is grown, it is the greatest among herbs,
and becometh a tree, so that the birds of the air come and lodge
in the branches thereof' [13:31–32].) In her reply to James D. Clark
in late 1882 – responding to his expression of sympathy after her
mother's death (and enclosure of something written by their dead
friend Charles Wadsworth) – she quoted a passage from another
parable, one that had made a deep impression: 'No verse in the
Bible has frightened me so much from a Child as "from him that
hath not, shall be taken even that he hath." Was it because it's dark
menace deepened our own Door?' (L788). She is quoting from one
of the parables reported by Mark ('For he that hath, to him shall be
given: and he that hath not, from him shall be taken even that which
he hath' [4:25]). She must also have been drawn to a neighboring
verse: 'And [Jesus] said unto [the twelve], "Unto you it is given to

know the mystery of the kingdom of God: but unto them that are without, all these things are done in parables"' (4:11). Dickinson frequently felt herself to be 'without' – one of the outsiders from whom 'shall be taken even that which he hath'; but in her most eloquent letters and poems she wrote as one who has penetrated the impenetrable mystery – and who must veil the mystery ('tell it slant – ') to reveal it.[18]

A modern commentator has suggested that some Old Testament parables 'are intended to be obscure in order to force thought, and they can only be understood by the discerning'; another commentator suggests, further, that a similar purpose may be behind Mark's parable (about 'he that hath' and 'he that hath not') – the one that so deeply impressed and disturbed Emily Dickinson.[19] In Proverbs, a book she admired and quoted from in letters to friends (L608 and L708), the sayings of Solomon are introduced with praise for their importance to those who are naive ('To give subtilty to the simple') and to those who are shrewd (a perceptive man will come 'To understand a proverb, and the interpretation; the words of the wise, and their dark sayings' [1:4, 5–6]). In both parables and proverbs, expression is distilled into words of great weight and power. In the Parable of the Sower, the word of the kingdom is likened to a seed sown in the wayside, in stony places, among thorns, in the good ground (Matthew 13:18–23; Mark 4:3–20; Luke 8:5–15).

It was in the Book of Revelation, the apocalyptic vision of John of Patmos, and in the mysticism of Saint John's Gospel that she found the most compelling signs of the word incarnate.[20] John of Patmos tells how, in a vision, he received and followed the instructions of a heavenly voice: 'And I took the little book out of the angel's hand, and ate it up; and it was in my mouth sweet as honey: and as soon as I had eaten it my belly was bitter. And he said unto me, Thou must prophesy again before many peoples, and nations, and tongues, and kings' (Rev. 10:10–11). Toward the end of her life, Dickinson translates and transforms this passage into a joyous hymn – in Watts's common metre:

> He ate and drank the precious Words –
> His Spirit grew robust –
> He knew no more that he was poor,
> Nor that his frame was Dust –
>
> He danced along the dingy Days

> And this Bequest of Wings
> Was but a Book – What Liberty
> A loosened spirit brings –
>
> (1587)

Revelation stands apart from all other books of the Bible in its extraordinary flights of prophetic vision and impassioned language; she singled it out for mention when she informed Higginson, in 1862, of the books she valued. Here, in eight lines, is the story of John, the expansion of his spirit, the transformation of dingy days into joyous strength – through the sacred book whose words he has eaten and drunk. There is deliberate ambiguity in the 'Bequest': it was his in the little book he ate; and he has left us, in *his* book, ours.[21]

Dickinson celebrated the 'loosened spirit' of John of Patmos; and she found also the profoundest meaning in the John of the Fourth Gospel. An undated prose fragment, that has survived in a transcript made by Sue, demonstrates the hold over her mind of the Fourth Evangelist's compelling doctrine of the Logos: 'The import of that Paragraph "The Word made Flesh[.]" Had he the faintest intimation Who broached it Yesterday! "Made Flesh and dwelt among us"' (PF4). John's pronouncement ('And the Word was made flesh, and dwelt among us, [and we beheld his glory, . . .] full of grace and truth' [1:14]) moved her to write a poem (like the prose fragment, also transcribed by Sue and left undated):

> A Word made Flesh is seldom
> And tremblingly partook
> Nor then perhaps reported
> But have I not mistook
> Each one of us has tasted
> With ecstasies of stealth
> The very food debated
> To our specific strength –
>
> A Word that breathes distinctly
> Has not the power to die
> Cohesive as the Spirit
> It may expire if He –
> "Made Flesh and dwelt among us["]
> Could condescension be

Like this consent of Language
This loved Philology
(1651)

A. M. Hunter has called John's words 'the crowning statement' of his prologue, 'something never said before by Jew or Greek'; and he reminds us, further, of its profound impact on Augustine who 'found all he wanted in the Greek philosophers – Plato and the rest – except this, that the Word became flesh'.[22] Dickinson's gloss moves from 'the Word' (from the manhood and ministry of Jesus, as reported by John) to our partaking of it – each of us according to our need and capacity ('our specific strength – '). John's unique contribution was to identify the word of God with the person of Christ – and, in the opening stanza, Dickinson describes the sacramental supper each of us, with greater or lesser awareness, feeds upon. ('In the beginning was the Word' – and it is soon made manifest that the Word made flesh in Christ's person must move toward and beyond the cross.) In the closing stanza, the poet's shift from the Word made flesh to 'A Word that breathes distinctly' is her tribute to man's sacred gift of language, to the sacred vocation of making poems.

The living word of a great poet 'Has not the power to die', cannot be separated from the Spirit, may die only if Christ ('Made Flesh and dwelt among us') dies. Christ lives – and the concluding unpunctuated lines convey the hope that God's 'condescension' (defined in her lexicon as a 'Voluntary descent from rank') can speak to us as powerfully as the deathless words of great poets. Dickinson's subjunctive mood ('Could condescension be') is used not to convey doubt but to undercut conventionally pious pronouncements. Dickinson transforms Watts's reverential hymn for the Lord's Supper ('Let us adore th' eternal Word / 'Tis he our souls hath fed:')[23] into an intimate and dramatic colloquy ('But have I not mistook / Each one of us has tasted') – in the *Sevens and Sixes* of the hymn book. Dickinson's intensely personal vision of the universe never completely relinquishes John's vision – or Watts's.[24]

According to Charles Anderson, 'A Word made Flesh is seldom' illustrates the 'miraculous power of language in the few great authors of her election'; Anderson further suggests that 'The symbols of the Eucharist and the doctrine of the Word were simply metaphors to express her passionate conviction about the power of poetry'.[25] Dickinson's sense of sacred vocation (discussed in the following chapter) encompassed a view of the miraculous power of language that retains a hold on John's doctrine of the Word; among the 'few great authors of her election' are those she could not fully follow – or fully leave behind: John of the Fourth Gospel, Thomas à Kempis, Herbert and Vaughan, Charles Wadsworth (in his sermons) and Thomas Wentworth Higginson (in his nature essays).

4

According to Martha Winburn England, Isaac Watts 'established a new relation between church song and scripture'. 'All attacks on his work', she observes, 'arose from his refusal to accept Scripture without altering it, from his determination to interpret its relevance to present experience'. Each one of his hymns, England suggests, 'is essentially an act of criticism, of interpretation'. Watts produced his vast collection of hymns alone, without authorisation or supervision by any church body – 'a shocking example of Protestant individualism' that, though insufficiently individualistic to Dickinson, seems to anticipate her approach a century and a half later. England finds those who define Dickinson's theological position as unconventionally mischievous or commendably audacious akin to the critics of Watts who praised or blamed him for threatening tradition, for testing doctrine by experience instead of experience by doctrine.[26]

Isaac Watts had been an important dimension of Dickinson's consciousness since her earliest childhood. She occasionally poked fun at his earnest pieties – but she found appealing his avoidance of exalted sentiment and language, his emphasis on homely dramatisation and colloquialism. William Allen's lengthy preface to his edition of *Psalms and Hymns for Public Worship* (Boston, 1835) provides a litany of complaints about Watts remarkably similar to the criticism later levelled against Dickinson. Allen regrets Watts's error in believing that devotion is promoted 'by grovelling thoughts, low images, or vulgarity of language'. He deplores his 'prosaic phraseology', his 'defective rhythm', his 'bad rhymes'. He quotes a recent critic who pointed out that Watts's age 'was not so nicely critical as the present; pure and perfect harmony was not so rigidly required . . . ' And Allen provides a long list of pairs of words that Watts mistakenly yokes as rhymes: secure, more; feet, straight;

stars, years; seeks, breaks; earth, breath; station, compassion – 'and hundreds of others but little more harmonious'.[27] Allen's criticism of Watts's crudities are paralleled, a half century later, in an anonymous British review of the first published collection of Emily Dickinson's poetry; the reviewer (who had American counterparts) complains about the bad rhymes in 'I taste a liquor never brewed' (pearl, alcohol) and insists that 'There are no words that can say how bad poetry may be when it is divorced from meaning, from music, from grammar, from rhyme; in brief, from articulate and intelligible speech'.[28] In Watts, Emily Dickinson had found a model both pious and adventurous – a kindred spirit who encouraged her own bold exploration and experimentation.[29]

New England hymnbooks were largely drawn from Isaac Watts's *The Psalms of David Imitated in the Language of the New Testament and Spiritual Songs*, completed in 1719. In 1830 – the year of Emily Dickinson's birth – there was a copy of *The Psalms of David Imitated* in every pew, schoolroom, and home; and 'Amherst was in the heart of a Watts enclave'.[30] These hymns, sung without accompaniment, were impressive; but in 1839 the church to which the Dickinsons belonged acquired a double bass viol. Austin Dickinson, then a boy of ten, would recall to the end of his life the haunting tones Josiah Ayres drew from its lower chords while accompanying the singing of some of Watts's *Favorite Hymns*.[31] That these tones and songs also haunted Emily is indicated by her comment, in an 1877 letter to Elizabeth Holland: 'How precious Thought and Speech are! "A present so divine," was in a Hymn they used to sing when I went to Church' (521). She is recalling, somewhat inaccurately, a line from the last stanza of Watts's 'When I survey the wondrous cross'.

The Dickinson household had copies of Watts's *Church Psalmody* and *The Psalms, Hymns, and Spiritual Songs* in its library. It is from these volumes that Emily Dickinson derived the metrical patterns (most frequently, common metre; occasionally, short and long metre) for most of her own 'hymns'. Each of the Watts hymns was identified by appropriate abbreviations (C. M., S. M., L. M.); a further system of vowel symbols was used to indicate tempo, from 'very slow' to 'very quick'; the same vowel symbols italicised designated the quantity of voice, from 'very soft' to 'very loud'; and the manner of expression (for example, 'pathetic', 'grand', or 'spirited') was designated by still other symbols. Dickinson's much discussed dashes clearly derive from Watts:

In the *Punctuation*, regard has been had to musical expression. In some instances, therefore, different points or pauses are inserted, from what would have been used, had the grammatical construction, only, been regarded. The *dash* is intended to denote an expressive suspension. In order to good expression, a distinct and judicious observance of the pauses, is absolutely necessary.[32]

A stanza from Watts's 'Behold the morning sun' illustrates how Dickinson uses Watts as a model – and as a springboard for her own distinctive creation. The Watts hymn is designated Short Metre ('S. M.') – with vowel symbols omitted, signifying 'common' tempo and degree of loudness:

> [Watts]
> My gracious God, how plain
> Are thy directions given!
> O may I never read in vain,
> But find the path to heaven.[33]

> [Dickinson]
> I never spoke with God
> Nor visited in Heaven –
> Yet certain am I of the spot
> As if the Checks were given –
> (1052, stanza 2)

There is a parallelism here – but also a striking divergence from Watts's supplicating and self-deprecating obeisance. Watts speaks directly to his great Lord on high, praises the clarity of his instructions, yearns uncertainly for his own worthiness to find the true path. Dickinson, in contrast, translates Watts's uncertain journey – through her comparison with a train trip – into a colloquial and forceful expression of unswerving faith. The idea of speaking with God (as if he were a neighbor) and visiting heaven (as if it were a neighborhood) would be more than slightly irreverent if it did not wittily emphasise the speaker's distance from God and heaven – an emphasis that vastly increases the force of the speaker's expression of faith in the closing lines. The last line ('As if the Checks were given') conveys concretely and colloquially the everyday experience of a railroad train traveller who surrenders his ticket to the conductor and receives in exchange a 'check' – a stub marked in such a way as to validate his journey to a designated place.[34]

The evangelical church hymns of Isaac Watts provided the firm understructure of fervent piety on which she builds astonishing structures – frequently probing and witty, frequently suggestive of a searching skepticism uncharacteristic of her hymn-writing mentor. But Watts's wry wit and homely imagery also occasionally fore-shadow Dickinson's; one of the hymns recalled by Austin Dickinson – and probably known to his sister – conveys some of her penetrating vision and sharp focus; it is in Long Metre and is marked 'e' (slow):

> Broad is the road that leads to death,
> And thousands walk together there;
> But wisdom shows a narrow path
> With here and there a traveller.[35]

In a related (though decidedly different) way, Dickinson conveys her thought about the many and the few – and the paths they travel; about the difficulty of discovering royal presences amidst the crowd:

> The life is thick – I know it!
> Yet – not so dense a crowd –
> But *Monarchs* – are *perceptible* –
> Far down the dustiest road!
> (270, stanza 4)

(Four decades later, Stephen Crane – a poet greatly influenced by Dickinson [and the son of a Methodist minister] – transformed Watts's stanza into a sardonic poem, 'The Wayfarer'; in it, a traveller observes that the pathway to truth is choked with weeds – but when he also sees that each weed is 'a singular knife' he concludes that 'Doubtless there are other roads'.)[36]

In another satiric echo of Watts's hymn, Dickinson sums up the difficulty of getting to heaven (in a poem incorporated into an 1880 letter to Elizabeth Holland):

> The Road to Paradise is plain
> And holds scarce one.
> Not that it is not firm
> But we presume
> A Dimpled Road
> Is more preferred

> The Belles of Paradise are few –
> Not me – nor you –
> But unsuspected things –
> Mines have no Wings.
>
> (L650)

Shira Wolosky sees in this parody of Watts's 'Broad is the road' a witty questioning not only of her own election but of an orthodox scheme of things in which trivial offenses lead to damnation.[37] Dickinson seems also to be satirising the trivialisation of God's mysterious ways.

In an early letter to Sue she quoted from the hymn setting of a Cowper poem ('God moves in a mysterious way, his wonders to perform') to joke about her transformation into a bear, in some future existence, to bite her fellow men ('it will be for the highest good of this fallen and perishing world' [L97]); the second stanza evoked 'unfathomable mines' – mines with wings:

> Deep in unfathomable mines
> Of never-failing skill,
> He treasures up his bright designs
> And works his sovereign will.[38]

But these were mines all too fathomable; she demanded profounder mysteries and brighter designs than those offered by Cowper or Watts.

5

A book greatly valued by Emily Dickinson and of great importance to the shaping of her personal life and development as a poet was Thomas à Kempis' *The Imitation of Christ*. This powerful and personal fifteenth-century redaction of Scripture was known to her through copies of the 1857 edition (presented to her by Sue that year or shortly thereafter) and the 1876 edition (presented, also by Sue, as a Christmas gift the year of its publication); both copies are marked in ways that indicate a significant familiarity and involvement.[39] The *Imitation* dwells on the central importance of the Lord's Supper – and the need for simplicity and purity in everyday life ('By two wings, a man is lifted up from things earthly, namely, by Simplicity and Purity').[40] An extraordinary poem, copied about 1859, seems a response to the *Imitation* as it dramatises the poet's struggle for faith – her struggle to become 'as little children' and, despite the conflicting evidences of nature, to receive the Body of Christ 'with all delight and spiritual eagerness':

> These are the days when Birds come Back –
> A very few – a Bird or two –
> To take a backward look.
>
> These are the days when skies resume
> The old – old sophistries of June –
> A blue and gold mistake.
>
> Oh fraud that cannot cheat the Bee –
> Almost thy plausibility
> Induces my belief.
>
> Till ranks of seeds their witness bear –
> And softly thro' the altered air
> Hurries a timid leaf.
>
> Oh Sacrament of summer days,
> Oh Last Communion in the Haze –
> Permit a child to join.
>
> Thy sacred emblems to partake –
> Thy consecrated bread to take
> And thine immortal wine!
>
> (130)

In the dying season, there is for the child – and for the child in spirit – the possibility and promise of eternal life. The lesson of the undeceived bee is that the season is indeed dying; the bee is not cheated in *this* false season. But they who become as little children partake in a celebration of cyclical death and life, of life in death – and are not cheated in any season. (After her father's death, Emily Dickinson quoted from Matthew 18:3 to inform a friend 'that Father had "Become as Litle Children"' [L425].)[41]

An important dimension of the *Imitation* that had special appeal to Dickinson dwelled on Christ's suffering and on the reluctance of his followers to share that suffering. Among the passages apparently marked by Dickinson is the following account of 'How Few are the Lovers of the Cross of Jesus':

> Jesus hath now many lovers of His heavenly kingdom,

but few bearers of His Cross.
He hath many desirous of consolation, but few of
tribulation.
He findeth many companions of His table, but few of
His abstinence.
All desire to rejoice with Him; few are willing to
endure anything for Him, or with Him.
Many follow Jesus unto the breaking of bread; but
few to the drinking of the Cup of His Passion.[42]

In numerous poems, most of them written during the crisis year
of 1862, Dickinson identifed herself with those who share Christ's
suffering on the cross.[43] But her approach is less that of the reverential worshipper than of one who sees among those around her
– and in herself – marvellous and terrible reenactments of Christ's
Passion:

> One Crucifixion is recorded – only –
> How many be
> Is not affirmed of Mathematics –
> Or History –
>
> One Calvary – exhibited to Stranger –
> As many be
> As Persons – or Peninsulas –
> Gethsemane –
>
> Is but a Province – in the Being's Centre –
> Judea –
> For Journey – Or Crusade's Achieving –
> Too near –
>
> Our Lord – indeed – made Compound Witness –
> And yet –
> There's newer – nearer Crucifixion
> Than That –
>
>   (553)[44]

The great repositories of knowledge (mathematics, history) cannot
tell us what the poem's persona informs us with authority: Experience provides the demonstration that learned disciplines cannot.

We need not make a pilgrimage to witness the place of Christ's suffering. We need only look within. The poem might seem to undermine the divine authority of the one recorded crucifixion – of Christ's unique sacrifice – by proclaiming a newer testament of nearer Gethsemanes.[45] Her profound admiration of Shakespeare, however, had not been undermined by her persona's pronouncement that 'Drama's Vitallest Expression is the Common Day' – that '"Hamlet" to Himself were Hamlet – / Had not Shakespeare wrote – ' (741). He was all the greater a guide because he unveiled truths readily available and visible in Amherst – truths that would enlarge her life and poems. She approached the sacred truths of the Bible and the *Imitation* in much the same way.

Jack Capps has linked an undated Dickinson poem (that has survived only in a transcript made by Mrs Todd) to the crucifixion imagery of the Bible and the *Imitation*:

> Proud of my broken heart, since thou didst break it
> Proud of the pain I did not feel till thee,
>
> Proud of my night, since thou with moons dost slake it,
> *Not* to partake thy passion, *my* humility.
>
> Thou can'st not boast like Jesus, drunken without companion
> Was the strong cup of anguish brewed for the Nazarene
>
> Thou can'st not pierce tradition with the peerless puncture.
> See! I usurped *thy* crucifix to honor mine!
> (1736)[46]

Dickinson's lexicon defines *passion* as 'Suffering; *emphatically*, the last suffering of the Savior'. The suffering of Jesus, as recounted by Matthew (26:42, 27:34) tells of his prayer – amidst his sleeping disciples ('if this cup may not pass away from me, except I drink it, thy will be done') – and, at Golgotha, of the vinegar and gall he is given to drink. The brokenhearted lover in the poem has not been permitted to share the 'passion' of her beloved – but she will not permit him to suffer, like Jesus, without a companion. His crucifix belongs as well to her.

There is no evidence for regarding this love poem as more than a metaphorical flight (an uncharacteristically halting and stilted one) – for linking it to the ordeal of her Master or the exile of her 'dearest earthly friend', the Reverend Charles Wadsworth. It is noteworthy, however, that the elegy on Wadsworth, 'Obtaining but his own extent' – discussed in the preceding chapter – links Wadsworth to Christ's suffering and Resurrection.

6

A heavily marked chapter in Dickinson's copy of the *Imitation* is titled 'Of the Love of Solitude and Silence' – and one of its marked sentences must have spoken with special force to the poet: 'The greatest Saints avoided the society of men, when they could conveniently, and did rather choose to live to God, in secret'.[47] Sir Thomas Browne, whose collected works were a part of the Dickinson family library, conveyed a similar view in his *Christian Morals*:

> He who must needs have company, must needs have sometimes bad company. Be able to be alone. Lose not the advantage of solitude, and the society of thyself; nor be only content, but delight to be alone and single with Omnipresency.[48]

Friendship and love play an important part in Browne's vision of 'the advantage of solitude'; in *Religio Laici*, he tells of the wonderful mystery of 'one soul in two bodies': 'There are wonders in true affection: it is a body of enigmas, mysteries, and riddles; wherein two so become one, as they both become two.'[49]

Even before she initiated her correspondence with Higginson, Emily Dickinson was engaged in a life that reflected Browne's vision of simultaneous solitude and deep involvement: She diligently dedicated herself to the making of poems; she carried on an extensive correspondence with those she valued – and the poems that she called her letters to the world were frequently woven into the texture of letters to friends; on rare occasion, she invited valued friends to her house. In 'The Soul Selects her own Society – ' Dickinson's persona conveys her own version of Browne's vision:

> The Soul selects her own Society –
> Then – shuts the Door –
> To her divine Majority –
> Present no more –
>
> Unmoved – she notes the Chariots – pausing –
> At her low Gate –
> Unmoved – an Emperor be kneeling

Upon her Mat –

I've known her – from an ample nation –
Choose One –
Then – close the Valves of her attention –
Like Stone –

(303)[50]

The poem dramatises, in its opening stanza, the effortless exclu-
sivity of the soul – defined in Dickinson's lexicon as not only the
'immortal substance in man', but also the 'animating principle or
part; as an able commander is the *soul* of an army'. The 'divine
Majority' of Dickinson's persona, in the opening stanza, may suggest the choice of a solitude attended by God – or by a Godly
mission; but the courtship imagery in the following stanzas seems
to move her closer to the 'wonders in true affection' spoken of
by Browne. She is unmoved by seemingly irresistible suitors and
makes her own inevitable choice. The stunning trope in the poem's
closing lines ('Then – close the Valves of her attention – / Like
Stone – ') further transforms the enraptured meditations of Thomas
à Kempis and Sir Thomas Browne. We are suddenly confronted
with the mysterious natural world of the stonelike bivalve – and the
physical presence of the poem's persona and the mysterious truth of
her unexplained decision.

In his *Atlantic* essay 'Letter to a Young Contributor', Higginson
had praised 'the vital vigor' of Andrew Marvell and Sir Thomas
Browne;[51] shortly after initiating a correspondence with Higginson
in response to that essay, Dickinson identified Browne as one of the
prose writers she especially valued (L261). She echoed, in some of
her poems, some of Browne's distinctive words and phrases; and
she seems to have been responsive to the lively wit and occasional
playfulness that irradiate his profound meditations on God and
nature.[52]

In a characteristic passage (from *Religio Medici*), Browne wittily
meditates on the large lessons to be learned from the tiniest creatures of God's handiwork:

> . . . what reason may not go to school to the wisdom of bees,
> ants, and spiders? what wise hand teacheth them to do what
> reason cannot teach us? Ruder heads stand amazed at those
> prodigious pieces of nature, whales, elephants, dromedaries, and
> camels; these, I confess, are the colossi and majestic pieces of

her hand: but in these narrow engines there is more curious mathematics; and the civility of these little citizens more neatly sets forth the wisdom of their Maker.[53]

Browne's 'little citizens' have their counterpart in Dickinson's numerous celebrations of 'Nature's People' – creatures of all kinds and sizes, with great emphasis on the world of insects. Browne envisions a classroom in which bees, ants, and spiders are our teachers – who convey wisdom not only about themselves but also about *their* teacher. In a poem that startlingly evokes a meadow in late summer (transformed into what seems an open-air chapel), Dickinson presents what might be called the lesson of the cricket:

> Further in Summer than the Birds
> Pathetic from the Grass
> A minor Nation celebrates
> It's unobtrusive Mass.
>
> No Ordinance be seen
> So gradual the Grace
> A pensive Custom it becomes
> Enlarging Loneliness
> Antiquest felt at Noon
> When August burning low
> Arise this spectral Canticle
> Repose to typify
>
> Remit as yet no Grace
> No Furrow on the Glow
> Yet a Druidic Difference
> Enhances Nature now
>
> (1068)

When he received a copy of the poem (in January 1866), Higginson pencilled a query in the margin: 'Insect-Sounds?'[54] When she sent the poem to another correspondent, Dickinson referred to it as 'My Cricket' (L813).

Both Browne and Dickinson were acquainted with Proverbs 6:6–8 and 30:24–28, in which the wisdom of insects (ants, locusts, spiders) is cited to deflate man's folly and pride. In 'Further in Summer than the Birds', nature's sermon is more subtle. The birds have been active throughout the spring and now, late in summer, an insect makes its presence known. Its mournful sound is evocative of many more ages than man has experienced. It evokes mankind ('A minor Nation') and its ancient Christian ritual ('It's unobtrusive Mass'); it makes its spectral song heard and felt imperceptibly and overpoweringly (like God's riddles and parables). His law (as conveyed in ritual) is not made visible but its power is experienced with a gradualness that enlarges our loneliness – makes us aware of other worlds. The result, however, is not despair but a renewed sense of God's presence and peace. Summer is at the full: the brightness of the season is at its height, the glowing fields still unplowed. But the cricket's spectral chant has signaled a 'Druidic Difference': summer is at the full and summer is dying. Dickinson's cricket is a reminder of death – and of rebirth (for seasons are cyclical). Though the poem is charged with the language and imagery of Christian ritual, it is fitting that the eerie and ancient song of the insect ('Antiquest felt at Noon') should lead us back to the dawn of man's history, to his earliest gods. (Dickinson's spectral song draws on Browne's view that nature's manifestations were 'the Scripture and Theology of the heathens'.)[55]

Sir Thomas Browne reached for truth wherever he could find it – on occasion, beyond Christian belief and authority; he wrote, in *Religio Medici*:

> The severe schools shall never laugh me out of the philosophy of Hermes, that this visible world is but a picture of the invisible, wherein as in a portrait things are not truly, but in equivocal shapes, and as they counterfeit some more real substance in that invisible fabric.[56]

Dickinson shared this view and paid her own tribute to the Hermetic books (attributed to the Egyptian philosopher Hermes Trismegistus and his followers) in 'Strong Draughts of Their Refreshing Minds' (711) – an eight-line poem applicable as well to the stimulating mind and art of Sir Thomas Browne.[57]

A recent commentary on *Religio Medici* describes it as 'not a theological treatise' but 'a prose-poem' – 'a touching self-portrait of a soul that has been plunged into doubts and fears, has joyed in mystery and paradox, and has meditated long on the nature of death'.[58] Dickinson's compressed structures and style are far removed from Browne's elaborate reasonings and baroque amplitude; but the characterisation of *Religio Medici* in the preceding sentence can as readily be applied to Emily Dickinson's poetry: Dickinson's metaphorical flights are certainly not to be taken literally – but they are, in her best poems, rooted in ideas that she took seriously – that we can and should take seriously.[59]

7

In *Religio Medici*, Sir Thomas Browne tells how he can cure vices (i.e., physical infirmities) with pills 'when they remain incurable by divinity'; he does not boast, he adds, but 'plainly say' that 'we all labour against our own cure, for death is the cure of all diseases'.[60] 'All but Death, can be Adjusted – ' (749) proclaims Dickinson's persona in one of her numerous poems about dying and death – poems that range from intimations of perpetual extinction to affirmations of faith in immortality. Her personae are, on occasion, the dead ('Because I could not stop for Death – '); someone at the point of death ('I heard a Fly buzz – when I died – '); an onlooker at a deathbed ('I've seen a Dying Eye').

Dickinson's poems about death and immortality are frequently an occasion to ponder on the great mystery (which must remain insoluble) – and on the state of her belief (which is subject to change). In his discussion of one of the greatest of these poems, 'The Last Night that She lived', Louis L. Martz praises Dickinson's 'deliberate, tough, unsparing analysis of the state of grief'; he finds special significance in the final line of the closing stanza:

> And We – We placed the Hair –
> And drew the Head erect –
> And then an awful leisure was
> Belief to regulate –
>
> (1100, stanza 7)

Martz calls it a masterful rendering of crisis and emotional stress – of the struggle of those left behind to maintain their faith. A variant of the final line reads 'Our faith to – regulate – '; the word *regulate*, Martz notes, is 'exactly right'. It points to a lifetime's effort to regulate her life for greater self-understanding and self-control, while confronting the mysteries of existence. Her quarrel, Martz believes, is not with God but with 'the Calvinistic vision of God whose arbitrary will violates her passionate belief in the value of each individual being'. Martz links Dickinson, in this quest and quarrel, to the meditative poetry of Donne, Herbert, Crashaw,

Vaughan: Like George Herbert's God, her Deity 'is one who never minds an honest disagreement or a "freckled" opinion'.[61]

Jack Capps has called attention to several marked lines from Herbert's 'The Church-Porch' (in Sue Dickinson's copy of *The Temple*) – lines that reflect Emily Dickinson's approach to life and to her religious quest:

> By all means use sometimes to be alone,
> Salute thy self: see what thy soul doth wear.'
> Dare to look in thy chest, for 'tis thine own:
> And tumble up and down what thou find'st there.[62]

These lines could serve as a motto for Emily Dickinson's adventurous self-exploration – and for her daring experiments in the making of poems. From the *Springfield Republican* for 28 October 1876, Dickinson copied the middle stanzas of Herbert's 'Mattens' – substituting for Herbert's more conventional punctuation her own characteristic capitals and dashes:

> My God – what is a Heart,
> Silver – or Gold – or precious Stone –
> Or Star – or Rainbow – or a part
> Of all these things – or all of them in one?
>
> My God – what is a Heart –
> That thou should'st it so eye and woo
> Pouring upon it all thy art
> As if that thou had'st nothing else to do – [63]

Punctuation aside, it is not surprising that Millicent Todd Bingham would – on discovering these stanzas among Dickinson's papers – publish them, in the first edition of *Bolts of Melody*, as Dickinson's poem; the daring conceit in the first stanza and the playful wit in the last line, as Capps has pointed out, could readily be found in either poet and Bingham's mistake – corrected in the second printing of her collection – is an understandable one.[64] God's mysterious way with the human heart is Dickinson's subject in numerous poems; in one of them, she toys, as in Herbert's 'Mattens', with the unfathomable complexity of God's creation – and with the one unalterable limitation that God puts on his creation:

> Maddest Heart that God created
> Cannot move a sod
> Pasted by the simple summer

On the Longed for Dead
(1288, stanza 2)

Herbert's playfulness about the wondrous complexity of God's creation, the heart, has its counterpart in Dickinson's meditation on the utter helplessness of even the wildest and most impetuous heart when confronted by God's unalterable decree.

In Herbert's 'Virtue' (a poem available to Dickinson in the family library copy of Griswold's *Sacred Poets of England and America*), the recurrent refrain in three succeeding stanzas is the inevitability of death – for the 'Sweet day!' for the 'Sweet rose!' for the 'Sweet spring!' Herbert's concluding stanza (as printed in Griswold's anthology) turns from pervasive death to the eternal life of the soul:

> Only a sweet and virtuous soul
> Like seasoned timber never gives;
> But though the whole world turns to a coal,
> Then chiefly lives.[65]

Dickinson's 'Longed for Dead' live on in Herbert's 'Virtue'.

On occasion, Dickinson also conveys a vision of hope for those who mourn and yearn for the beloved dead:

> The Heart has many Doors –
> I can but knock –
> For any sweet "Come in"
> Impelled to hark –
> Not saddened by repulse,
> Repast to me
> That somewhere, there exists,
> Supremacy –
>   (1567)

This is one of the tributes to her dead nephew that she sent to Sue – kept by Sue among the many messages of condolence sent to her after Gilbert's death.[66] Here Dickinson draws on Matthew 7:7 ('knock, and it shall be opened') and Revelation 3:20 ('Behold, I stand at the door, and knock') to evoke God's magical and mysterious creation, the heart – to translate Herbert's celebration of the heart in 'Mattens' into her own distinctive response to a crushing loss. Dickinson's persona is impelled to look within her own chest (as Herbert dares us to do in 'The Church-Porch') to discover a heart with many doors – to find the one door that may open to 'the Longed for Dead'. She knocks, and it is not opened – but she is nourished by the awareness of a supreme presence. The sturdy colloquialism of the opening lines in 'The Heart has many Doors – ' is reinforced by its strikingly compact hymn metre (*Sixes and Fours*, a variation on *Sixes and Fives*) – a compactness culminated by the single polysyllabic word 'Supremacy – ' that constitutes the closing line. The informal immediacy of the first part of the poem is tempered, in the following lines, by archaisms (*hark, repulse, Repast*) that distance her from both the loved one she is vainly reaching for and the supreme being whose remote but certain existence helps to sustain her.

In Henry Vaughan, she found another kindred spirit – a poet who reinforced both her need to question and her need to believe.[67] Lines from Vaughan's 'Early Rising and Prayer' are echoed in Dickinson's 'A Little East of Jordan' (59); and she quotes from his 'They are all gone into the world of light!' in a letter to Higginson conveying sympathy on the death of his infant daughter (L653). Although there is no evidence that she read Vaughan's poems dealing with the English civil war, Dickinson's response to war (discussed in the following chapter) has much in common with his response. An elegy by Vaughan, written for a friend killed at the battle of Rowton Heath, opens on a note of defiance and rebellion: 'I Am Confirm'd, and so much wing is given / To my wild thoughts that they dare strike at heav'n.' He hopes that the lines that he inscribes to his dead friend may keep alive the memory of one who was noble and courageous – a memory that might enlarge the faith of a future, better time.[68] The poet struggles with his sense of rebellion and loss – and finds a way out of his grief and despair. Such strugglings and moments of despair are part of a lifelong quest for inner peace – for what Martz has called 'the paradise within'. In his comment on Vaughan's 'Rules and Lessons', stanzas offering spiritual counsel for troubled times, Martz might also be referring to Emily Dickinson: ' . . . Vaughan's advice bears no relation to any ecclesiastical symbolism: it is as though the earthly church had vanished and man were left to work alone with God'.[69]

In the *Springfield Republican* for 12 February 1863, was printed a stanza from 'Rules and Lessons' – in an article on 'Henry Vaughan and His Poems' – that spoke directly to Emily Dickinson's condition:

Seek not the same steps with the crowd; stick thou

> To thy sure trot; a constant, humble mind
> Is both his own joy and his Maker's too;
> Let folly dust it on, or lag behind, –
> *A sweet self – privacy in a right soul*
> Outruns the earth, and lines the utmost pole.[70]

Later in that same troubled year, Dickinson conveyed a similar declaration of spiritual independence:

> On a Columnar Self –
> How ample to rely
> In Tumult – or Extremity –
> How good the Certainty
>
> That Lever cannot pry –
> And Wedge cannot divide
> Conviction – That Granitic Base –
> Though None be on our Side –
>
> Suffice Us – for a Crowd –
> Ourself – and Rectitude –
> And that Assembly – not far off
> From furthest Spirit – God –
>   (789)[71]

Judith Banzer finds in the concluding stanza 'the kernel of her life and art'.[72] A year earlier, in April 1862, Emily Dickinson had found in Thomas Wentworth Higginson's *Atlantic* essay 'Letter to a Young Contributor' an affirmation of spiritual independence (in time of war) akin to that of Vaughan's – and had responded by initiating a correspondence of momentous importance to herself, to him, to us.

3

Singing Off Charnel Steps: Lessons for a Preceptor

Central among the sacred texts transformed by Emily Dickinson for her poetic purposes were the King James Version of the Bible and the hymns of Isaac Watts. The martial imagery prevalent in Dickinson's poems, early and late, was a pervasive presence in the Bible and in Watts – familiar to her from childhood on.[1] A hymn by Watts titled 'Holy Fortitude; or, The Christian Soldier' includes stanzas that provide an answer to an opening question ('Am I a soldier of the cross?'):

> Sure I must fight, if I would reign;
> Increase my courage, Lord;
> I'll bear the toil, endure the pain,
> Supported by thy word.
>
> Thy saints, in all this glorious war,
> Shall conquer, though they die;
> They view the triumph from afar,
> And seize it with their eye.[2]

Watts's hymn is listed, in the 'New Index of Subjects' prepared for the 1834 edition owned by Edward Dickinson, under the heading: 'Warfare, spiritual.'[3]

Several early Dickinson poems, written a few years before the outbreak of the war, dramatise the idea of spiritual victory through mortal trial – dramatise the ordeal of those who 'view the triumph from afar' and 'conquer, though they die'. In a poem that links blessed martial courage to earthly travail, Dickinson's persona

seems to anticipate the pomp and ceremony that would come to
Amherst when young Frazar Stearns, the son of the President of
Amherst College, was killed in action at the battle of Newbern:

> Bless God, he went as soldiers,
> His musket on his breast –
> Grant God, he charge the bravest
> Of all the martial blest!
>
> Please God, might I behold him
> In epauletted white –
> I should not fear the foe then –
> I should not fear the fight!
>
> (147)[4]

Her prayer of thanksgiving is not only for one who has courageously
joined the fight but also for herself: Could she but see him in his
transformed state, she might then find the courage to carry on
her fight.

This prayer for one who has finished his life struggle and death
struggle, written about 1858, deploys language and imagery linked
to Watts's 'Holy Fortitude' – and other hymns listed under the
heading *'Warfare*, spiritual'. Dickinson's famous 'Success is counted
sweetest' (67) makes similar use of Watts's martial rhetoric:

> Success is counted sweetest
> By those who ne'er succeed.
> To comprehend a nectar
> Requires sorest need.
>
> Not one of all the purple Host
> Who took the Flag today
> Can tell the definition
> So clear of victory
>
> As he defeated – dying –
> On whose forbidden ear
> The distant strains of triumph
> Burst agonized and clear![5]

'For the dying soldier', Richard Wilbur has observed, ' . . . defeat
and death are attended by an increase of awareness, and material
loss has led to spiritual gain'.[6]

The connections Dickinson's persona envisioned between mortal battlefield losses and eternal heavenly gains are linked, in still another early poem, to an invisible battleground of personal anguish:

> To fight aloud, is very brave –
> But *gallanter*, I know
> Who charge within the bosom
> The Cavalry of Wo –
>
> Who win, and nations do not see –
> Who fall – and none observe –
> Whose dying eyes, no Country
> Regards with patriot love –
>
> We trust, in plumed procession
> For such, the Angels go –
> Rank after Rank, with even feet –
> And Uniforms of Snow.
>
> (126)[7]

The unseen heroism of private suffering surpasses that to be found on any visible battlefield. Those who charge on the battlefield of the heart ('The Cavalry of Wo – ') will, the speaker hopes and believes, receive a recognition and reward in heaven not given them on earth.

Curtis Dahl has identified an added dimension in this poem that moves it beyond conventional religious sentiment and expression: Dickinson's poem is, among other things, a subtle transmutation of Tennyson's galloping lines celebrating the gallant, futile, fatal charge of the Light Brigade. In Dickinson's version, there is still a battle, a cavalry charge, a grand spectacle of heroic death – but now, Dahl suggests, 'Tennyson's outward heroic action has been internalized into an image of the lonely soul's unnoticed though agonizing struggle with itself'.[8]

The war had not yet visited Amherst when she wrote 'To fight aloud, is very brave – ' In the spring of 1861, the Civil War became a more pervasive presence in isolated Amherst. A week after the surrender of Fort Sumter, a sermon was preached in the college chapel 'in a strain intended to inspire courage, heroism, and self-sacrificing devotion'; after the sermon, a hundred students volunteered to enlist in a company being formed by Professor William Smith Clark (soon to be Colonel Clark).[9] Two months later, in early July, President Stearns delivered his commencement day sermon – an annual event at the Dickinson Homestead. In this time of national crisis, he offered a message of hope:

> There is progress in our land; all the forces of selfish and irresponsible power are mustering, that they may confederate and be broken . . . . We cannot always see the immediate results of any struggle, but we may be sure that God is on the side of Theism against idolatry, on the side of liberty against despotism, and in the end right must prevail.[10]

During this same period, Emily Dickinson was experiencing a great personal crisis: She wrote two impassioned letters to her Master ('Oh – did I offend it', in early 1861, and 'If you saw a bullet', in the summer of 1861); she was responding to the gathering storm of war in a far darker mood than that of President Stearns.

2

The numerous letters that Emily Dickinson wrote to her Norcross cousins have survived only in transcripts copied out and transmitted by them to Mabel Loomis Todd for her 1894 edition of the poet's letters. Among them are seven extracts placed together by Mrs Todd and dated 'Spring, 1861'. The last of these extracts makes an explicit reference to the war ('When did the war really begin?'); in another of them she seems to be reflecting on the war's terrible and incomprehensible toll – and on God's indifference to man's suffering:

> . . . The seeing pain one can't relieve makes a demon of one. If angels have the heart beneath their silver jackets, I think such things could make them weep, but Heaven is so cold! It will never look kind to me that God, who causes all, denies such little wishes. It could not hurt His glory, unless it were a lonesome kind. I 'most conclude it is. (L234)[11]

The following spring, in mid-March of 1862 (shortly before Wadsworth set sail for California and his new pastorate at Calvary Church), Dickinson's response to pain was put to an even more terrible test.

On 16 March 1862, Lieutenant Frazar A. Stearns, son of President Stearns, was killed in action at Newbern. The townspeople of Amherst – Austin and Emily Dickinson among them – were stunned

by the news. Eight months earlier, President Stearns had prophesied, in his commencement day sermon, the inevitable triumph of
justice and righteousness in the land; now, in a memorial volume
compiled to honor the fallen hero, the bereaved father wrote: 'He
fell doing his duty as a Christian soldier, and I am satisfied.' God,
in his wisdom, could not answer prayer for Frazar's preservation;
but God was now providing inward strength to those left behind.
President Stearns urges all to heed Christ's message to his followers
(John 16:33): 'In the world ye shall have tribulation, but be of good
cheer; I have overcome the World.'[12]

Emily Dickinson's deeply troubled response to the death of young
Frazar Stearns is very different from the Christian resignation and
'good cheer' advocated by his father. In a letter to Samuel Bowles,
she conveys Austin's deep distress over 'Frazer's murder' – a
distress that seems also to have been her own:

> Austin is chilled – By Frazer's murder – He says – his Brain keeps
> saying over "Frazer is killed" – "Frazer is killed," just as Father
> told it – to Him. Two or three words of lead – that dropped so
> deep, they keep weighing –
> Tell Austin – how to get over them! (L256)[13]

At about the same time, Dickinson sent to her Norcross cousins
a lengthy and detailed account of Frazar's dying moments in a
comrade's arms on the battlefield (asking twice for water and finally
murmuring 'My God!'); the circumstances surrounding the return of
the body to Amherst; the expressions of grief at the funeral by family
and villagers. St Armand finds in Dickinson's extraordinary account
a 'terse retelling of the passion according to Saint Matthew, as Frazar
cries out for water, questions his god, suffers on the cross of war,
and becomes the rigid centerpiece of a military pietà'. St Armand
suggests that Stearns 'had somehow become a symbol of her own
assassinated selfhood'; her account of young Frazar's death, his
heart shot away by a minie ball, parallels that of her own 'murder',
vividly described in a letter to her Master (written in the summer of
1861) about a bird hit by a bullet: 'One drop more from the gash that
stains your Daisy's bosom – then would you *believe?*'[14]

This parallel is reinforced, in Dickinson's account of young
Frazar's death and transfiguration, by a curious touch that transforms the dead youth's funeral procession through Amherst into
the charge of the Light Brigade on the plains of Balaclava: 'Just as
he fell, in his soldier's cap, with his sword at his side [she wrote to

her cousins], Frazer rode through Amherst. Classmates to the right of him, and classmates to the left of him, to guard his narrow face!' (L255) In Dickinson's version, protective classmates are substituted for the cannon that volleyed and thundered to the right and to the left of the doomed cavalrymen. In Tennyson's poem, all the world honors the wild charge of the noble six hundred and their unfading glory.[15] Dickinson tells how Frazar's unfading glory was similarly honored in Amherst: 'Crowds came to tell him good-night, choirs sang to him, pastors told how brave he was – early-soldier heart.' One of the pastors, Frazar's father, wrote in the memorial volume honoring his son: 'And why should not friends be satisfied when their fallen sons and brothers have died trusting in God and doing their duty?'[16] It is clear, however, that Dickinson could not share Tennyson's view of the slaughter at Balaclava – could not be satisfied about Frazar's fall, about the fall of thousands of young men on battlefields throughout the land. To her cousins, her last words about Frazar are not about God and duty but about love: 'Let us love better, children, it's most that's left to do.' And her last word, in a poem she may have written in response to Frazar's death, dwells finally not on God or duty or love – but on 'Murder'.

'Frazer is killed' was the deadly refrain that Austin's brain kept repeating, the poet informed Bowles; 'Austin is chilled – by Frazer's murder – ' (L256). Thomas H. Johnson has pointed to a poem, apparently written on the occasion of the death of young Stearns, that echoes the words of her letter to Bowles; it opens with an account of her persona's turbulent brain, her struggle to accept the fact of a sudden death and to make sense of that fact:

> It dont sound so terrible – quite – as it did –
> I run it over – "Dead", Brain, "Dead."
> Put it in Latin – left of my school –
> Seems it dont shriek so – under rule.

The stanzas that follow tell how the passage of time will help blunt the horror – but the closing stanza addresses itself, ironically, to an even more horrifying question:

> It's shrewder then
> Put the Thought in advance – a Year –
> How like "a fit" – then –
> Murder – wear!
>   (426)[17]

In the words of Thomas L. Ford, 'Should one adjust to death in war? Is it proper to make a nice "fit" out of something that is actually a form of murder?' Ford suggests that 'In the word *murder* [Dickinson] bitterly sums up her attitude toward war'.[18]

She pays tribute to the heroic dead in 'It feels a shame to be Alive – ' (444) while posing disturbing questions about an unheroic world that requires such terrible sacrifice:

> The price is great – Sublimely paid –
> Do we deserve – a Thing –
> That lives – like Dollars – must be piled
> Before we may obtain?
>
> Are we that wait – sufficient worth –
> That such Enormous Pearl
> As life – dissolved be – for Us –
> In Battle's – horrid Bowl?
>
> (stanzas 3 and 4)[19]

The 'thing' for which the great price is being sublimely paid is 'Liberty'; Dickinson's images (corpses stacked up like dollars, an enormous pearl of life dissolved in a horrid bowl) are far removed from Tennyson's flashing and heroic images in 'The Charge of the Light Brigade'.

And they are far removed from the fiery images in Julia Ward Howe's 'Battle Hymn of the Republic' – images that would reinforce the sentiments shared by Northern churchmen, including Wadsworth and Higginson, about the holy and righteous cause for which the young men of the nation would be shedding their blood:

> I have read a fiery gospel, writ in burnished rows of
> steel:
> "As ye deal with my contemners, so with you my grace
> shall deal;
> Let the Hero, born of woman, crush the serpent with
> his heel,
> Since God is marching on."[20]

The gospel Dickinson valued was neither fiery nor writ in burnished rows of steel; the God of Howe's hymn was not one Dickinson could celebrate.

Julia Ward Howe's fiery hymn appeared on the opening page of the *Atlantic Monthly* for February 1862; sung to the tune of 'John Brown's Body', it became the rallying cry of Union soldiers in the camps and on the march. Soon after its appearance in late January, Thomas Wentworth Higginson wrote to Editor James T. Fields and offered some candid comments about the shortcomings of the number. He called attention to a 'direful misprint' in his own contribution to it (the nature essay 'Snow') – and complained further about the absence of a strong essay on the war ('For the "Atlantic" to speak only once in three months, and then *against* an emancipatory policy, is humiliating'). He might have submitted one himself, he informed Fields, 'but I could not write when busy about regiments and companies . . . . ' Higginson enclosed in his letter an essay that he *had* found time to write, 'Letter to a Young Contributor'.[21]

In fact, Higginson was, at the time he wrote to Fields, in the midst of a profound personal crisis – a crisis over his ambivalent feelings about the conflicting claims on him of an invalid wife and a nation at war. He had become a regular contributor to *Atlantic Monthly* when it was founded in 1858; his numerous articles on anti-slavery issues and women's rights contributed to his reputation as an ardent activist. There was also another side to Higginson (especially appealing to Emily Dickinson), one that most clearly emerged in mid-1861, after a temporary discouragement in his plan to form a regiment: He had a longstanding passion for nature studies and, in the words of Tilden G. Edelstein, 'Being a commander without a military command moved him to direct his *Atlantic* articles to nature's regiments of flora and fauna'. After spending many hours observing insects and birds, he wrote in his field book: 'I burn with insatiable desire to penetrate their consciousness'; in another entry he told how pleased he was to 'come back to the one thing which I have always enjoyed, a quiet life with literature and nature'. The nature essays that Higginson wrote for the *Atlantic* earned him the praise of, among others, Thoreau; they aroused even greater enthusiasm in Emily Dickinson. These included, in 1861–2, 'My Out-Door Study', 'Snow', 'The Life of Birds', 'The Procession of the Flowers'.[22] 'Letter to a Young Contributor', submitted in January 1862 and printed in the April *Atlantic*, was closely attuned to these meditative studies of nature.

Higginson's ambivalent feelings about participating in the war were finally resolved in the midst of mounting war excitement; in early August, he wrote in his diary that he had finally 'decided that I never could hold up my head again . . . if I didn't vindicate my past words by actions, though tardy'.[23] After a three-month stint as captain of a Massachusetts company, Higginson accepted an invitation to take command of the first black regiment in the Union army, being recruited from freed slaves at Port Royal, South Carolina; Colonel Higginson left Worcester for South Carolina and his new post in mid-November of 1862.[24]

When it appeared in the April *Atlantic*, Higginson's 'Letter to a Young Contributor' had an electrifying effect on Emily Dickinson. She initiated a correspondence, on 15 April, that continued until her death – a correspondence of momentous importance to them both. (Anna Mary Wells has pointed out that 'She had never before sent an unsolicited letter to a stranger, and she was never to do so again'.)[25] By July, they had exchanged four letters; when Dickinson received no reply to her fifth letter – written in August, the month in which Higginson's vacillation over the war was finally resolved – she sent him, on 6 October, an urgent plea: 'Did I displease you, Mr Higginson? But wont you tell me how?'(L274) The author of 'Letter to a Young Contributor' had spoken directly to her and the sacred calling she had chosen; she, in turn, had much to teach him during and after the war that for a time engulfed them both.

3

Fifteen years after the appearance of 'Letter to a Young Contributor', Dickinson reminded Higginson of a sentence from it that had helped sustain her: 'Such being the Majesty of the Art you presume to practice, you can at least take time before dishonoring it . . . . '[L488]) St Armand has observed that it was 'Higginson's nearness to nature and his high exaltation that prompted Dickinson to choose him as a confidant'; his reverent approach to nature and to the art of writing about nature reinforced her own.[26] But there is an additional explanation for the profound impact this essay had on the poet: Higginson's reputation as a militant abolitionist was widely known; the note he sounded in his 'Letter to a Young Contributor', however, was one of renunciation of the swirling passions of the time for higher, more permanent rewards:

Once the poets and the sages were held to be pleasing triflers, fit for hours of relaxation in the lulls of war. Now the pursuits of peace are recognized as the real, and war as the accidental. It interrupts all higher avocations, as does the cry of fire: when the fire is extinguished, the important affairs of life are resumed.[27]

Other aspects of Higginson's essay must also have struck home: His plea for compression ('there may be years of crowded passion in a word, half a life in a sentence'); his warning against hasty writing; his emphasis on patient and painstaking revision.[28] This was counsel that reinforced the commitment she had already made to herself and to her sacred calling.

Even more compelling must have been the concluding paragraph of 'Letter to a Young Contributor'; to a poet who was celebrating, in numerous poems, her persona's mystical marriage to a Man of God (and depicting her persona's troubled search for God), Higginson spoke with irresistible force:

> Yet, if our life be immortal, this temporary distinction [between fame and oblivion] is of little moment, and we may learn humility, without learning despair, from earth's evanescent glories. Who cannot bear a few disappointments, if the vista be so wide that the mute inglorious Miltons of this sphere may in some other sing their Paradise as Found? War or peace, fame or forgetfulness, can bring no real injury to one who has formed the fixed purpose to live nobly day by day. I fancy that in some other realm of existence we may look back with some kind interest on this scene of our earlier life, and say to one another, – 'Do you remember yonder planet, where once we went to school?' And whether our elective study here lay chiefly in the fields of action or of thought will matter little to us then, when other schools shall have led us through other disciplines.[29]

For Higginson, a belief in an afterlife, in the evanescence of earth's glories, in the permanent glory of a fixed purpose, in another and higher 'realm of existence' – all these were deep convictions that remained with him throughout his career as a Unitarian minister and after he left the pulpit. (In an 1859 lecture, 'The Results of Spiritualism' [discussed in the following chapter], Higginson hailed the rise of a movement that was restoring man's instinctively held faith in the never-ending relation between 'the other world and this' – that was undermining gloomy orthodox Christian pronouncements about 'a gloomy sleep of ages and an incredible resurrection to end it.')[30] 'You mention Immortality', wrote Dickinson to Higginson in

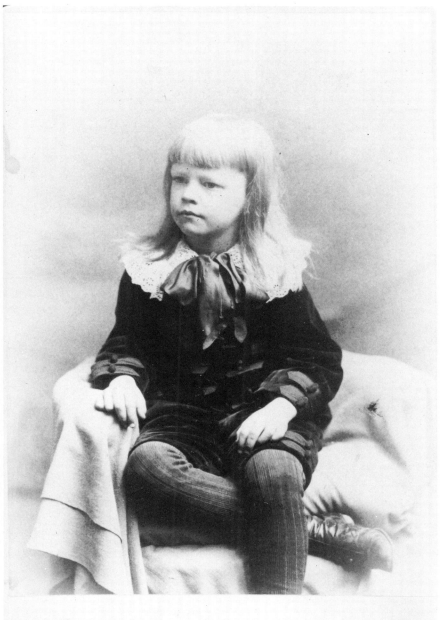

1. Thomas Gilbert Dickinson.

2. Reverend Charles Wadsworth.

4. Maria Whitney.

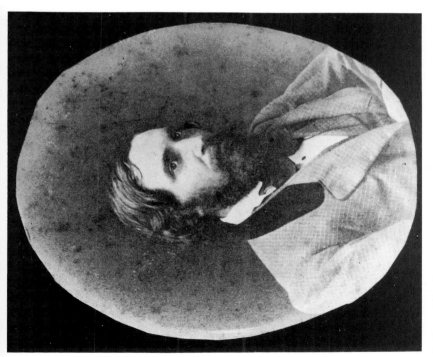

3. Samuel Bowles.

5. Adjutant Frazar Stearns.

6. Letter from Emily Dickinson to Thomas Wentworth Higginson, 15 April 1862.

7. Thomas Wentworth Higginson.

8. Edward Dickinson, 1874.

9. Thomas Wentworth Higginson and his daughter, Margaret, 1885.

1866; 'That is the Flood subject' (L319). It was the 'Flood subject' for them both and its pervasive presence helps explain the lifelong bond between them.

The opening sentence of Dickinson's famous first letter of 15 April ('Are you too deeply occupied to say if my Verse is alive?') was a response to Higginson's call, in his *Atlantic* essay, for language 'saturated with warm life'; she would be grateful to learn from him whether 'it breathed' – and would feel honor toward him for a candid verdict if it did not (L260); she enclosed four poems: 'Safe in their Alabaster Chambers', 'The nearest Dream recedes unrealized', 'We play at Paste', and 'I'll tell you how the Sun rose'. (Thirty years later, Higginson told of the profound impression this letter and these poems had made of poetic genius – yoked to the problem, still unsolved for him, of the place to assign in literature to this unconventional and elusive voice.)[31]

Higginson promptly responded to this remarkable communication from Amherst with criticism of the poems and curiosity about the poet. His letter has not survived (with two exceptions, Higginson's numerous letters seem to have been destroyed after the poet's death) but her answer tells us that he has provided critical comments about her poems ('Thank you for the surgery – ') and asked questions about herself, her books, her friends. Dickinson's answer fuses serious confiding and incisive wit: She tells of her personal crisis ('I had a terror – since September – I could tell to none – '); her reading ('For Poets – I have Keats – and Mr and Mrs Browning. For Prose – Mr Ruskin – Sir Thomas Browne – and the Revelations'); her companions ('Hills – Sir – and the Sundown – and a Dog – large as myself'). She provides a humorous family portrait, with deft strokes for her mother (who 'does not care for thought') and father (who 'buys me many Books – but begs me not to read them – because he fears they joggle the Mind') – and for both her parents' religious orthodoxy ('They are religious – except me – and address an Eclipse every morning – whom they call their "Father"' [L261]). Dickinson may have been responding, in part, to Higginson's witty commentary, in an earlier *Atlantic* essay, on the subjection of women in our society – and on the ever-increasing signs of change ('Who believed [wrote Higginson] that a poetess could ever be more than an Annot Lyle of the harp, to soothe with sweet melodies the leisure of her lord, until in Elizabeth Barrett's hands the thing became a trumpet?')[32]

Dickinson concluded her next letter with a question: 'But, will you be my Preceptor, Mr Higginson?'(L265) and, until her death put an end to their correspondence twenty-four years later, almost invariably closed her letters by calling herself 'Your Scholar – ' But Dickinson's Preceptor soon learned that his friendship was more greatly valued than his counsel – that he was much more *her* Scholar than she was his. In a poem she enclosed in her first letter, 'The nearest Dream recedes unrealized', Dickinson compares the pursuit of this dream to a boy chasing an elusive June bee; thirty years later, in his *Atlantic* essay on their correspondence, Higginson quotes the poem and observes: 'The bee himself did not evade the schoolboy more than she evaded me; and even at this day I still stand somewhat bewildered, like the boy.'[33]

'Are these more orderly?' she asked in her fifth letter (in August 1862). 'I think you called me "Wayward." Will you help me improve?'(L271) (Higginson later told how he quickly abandoned his efforts 'to lead her in the direction of rules and tradition' – how he soon realized how much more she interested him in her 'unregenerate condition'.)[34] He could not help her to improve – but could and would help her, in her time of great need, to survive. His approach to literature was too conventional to allow him to take a full measure of her original power – but he was drawn despite himself and had intimations of its extraordinary dimensions.

Higginson had answered each one of her first four letters promptly; after waiting for several weeks for a reply to her fifth letter, Dickinson wrote again, this time with disquietude: 'Did I displease you Mr Higginson? But wont you tell me how?'(L274) She had not displeased him and she eventually learned that her Preceptor was during this time too deeply occupied with war matters to respond to her letters. An item in the *Springfield Republican* on 4 December brought the news that Higginson (who had been serving as captain of an Army company in Worcester since August) had accepted a new command as colonel of a black regiment in South Carolina;[35] this item appeared just days after the publication in the December *Atlantic* of Higginson's extraordinary nature essay 'The Procession of the Flowers'. When an additional commentary on Colonel Higginson and his regiment appeared in the *Republican* in early February, Dickinson wrote again to her Preceptor to convey concern about his current confrontation with death at the front – and to note, in a postscript, a connection between nature's message, in his *Atlantic* essay, and his present danger.

'War feels to me an oblique place – ' she informs Higginson; and she asks: 'Should there be other Summers, would you perhaps come?' Death, 'striking sharp and early', has infused her love for friends more with 'alarm, than peace'; she trusts he will survive the war – 'and though not reared to prayer – when service is had in Church, for Our Arms, I include yourself – ' In his *Atlantic* essay, Higginson had pointed out how 'There is always some single chosen nook, which you might cover with your handkerchief, where each flower seems to bloom earliest, without variation, year by year'.[36] She tells him that 'I, too, have an "Island" – whose "Rose and magnolia" are in the Egg . . . . ' His essay and her own observations move her to the thought 'that the "Supernatural," was only the Natural, disclosed – ' And she adds a two-line poem:

> Not "Revelation" – 'tis – that waits,
> But our unfurnished eyes –

She also enclosed a longer poem, 'The Soul unto itself' (683); and the letter closes with a postscript: 'I trust the "Procession of Flowers" was not a premonition – ' (L280)

Dickinson's postscript may be referring to the cycle of life vividly depicted in Higginson's essay: Autumn is signalled by the Barrel-Gentian at the roadside – and the Mourning Cloak Moth in the meadows 'gives coincident warning'; on the water, the last water lilies sink beneath the surface. Higginson cites Harriet Prescott's view 'that some souls are like the Water-Lilies, fixed, yet floating. But others are like [the rootless plants of the delicate Bladder-Wort], floating unfixed, kept in place only by its fellows around it, until perhaps a breeze comes, and, breaking the accidental cohesion, sweeps them all away'. And Dickinson may also be referring to a passage in which two opposing views are presented: ' . . . we are bidden, on high authority, to love the wood-rose and leave it on its stalk; but against this may be set the saying of Bettine, that "all flowers which are broken become immortal in the sacrifice . . . . "'[37] Her ten-word postscript sums up all these intimations of mortality and immortality in 'The Procession of the Flowers' – and in the war that Higginson was confronting.[38]

Just about the time she was writing to Higginson about the war and his *Atlantic* essay there appeared in the *Springfield Republican* the article on 'Henry Vaughan and His Poems' (discussed earlier, in Chapter Two); the article concludes by quoting the last six stanzas of 'The Seed growing secretly'. The first of these stanzas could have served as an epigraph to 'The Procession of the Flowers':

> Dear, secret *Greenness*! nurst below
> Tempests and windes, and winter-nights
> Vex not, that but one sees thee grow,
> That *One* made all these lesser lights.

The following stanzas quoted in the *Republican* point to the conflicting claims of 'Glory, the Crouds cheap tinsel' and the permanent truths of God's natural growth. And the concluding stanza emphasises the need to foster this 'secret growth' within ourselves for true fulfillment in life and in death:

> Then bless thy secret growth, nor catch
> At noise, but thrive unseen and dumb;
> Keep clean, bear fruit, earn life and watch,
> Till the white winged Reapers come![39]

Vaughan's reapers are the angels in the parable of the good seed and the tares of the field (Matthew 13:39). Vaughan's vision of man's triumphant independence – of his link to nature and to God – was occasionally clouded, especially during the English civil war, by bitterness and doubt. Dickinson's suffering over the departure of her beloved minister because of the war, her concern about her Preceptor's dangerous involvement, her horror over the slaughter on the battlefields, her awareness of the war fever gripping the nation (and Amherst) – all these feelings are incorporated into poems that reflect a similar struggle to keep intact 'a Columnar Self – / . . . / In tumult – or Extremity – ' (789).

One such poem, enclosed in the letter she sent to Higginson as he prepared for battle in South Carolina, deploys martial imagery to depict the strategies of a soul seeking to undermine itself:

> The Soul unto itself
> Is an imperial friend –
> Or the most agonizing Spy –
> An Enemy – could send –
>
> Secure against it's own –
> No treason it can fear –
> Itself – it's Sovreign – of itself
> The Soul should stand in Awe –
> (683)[40]

The deadly maneuverings of the battlefield serve as a trope in this study of divine selfhood teetering on the brink of self-destruction.

In another poem the slaughter on the battlefield is treated as a manifestation of nature; and the dead who have disappeared from sight are still visible to God. But nature here evokes, instead of God's plenitude and cyclical scheme, a vast meaningless violence; and there is little comfort in knowing that the dead, lost forever to mortal view, are still visible to God:

> They dropped like Flakes –
> They dropped like Stars –
> Like Petals from a Rose –
> When suddenly across the June
> A Wind with fingers – goes –
>
> They perished in the Seamless Grass –
> No eye could find the place –
> But God can summon every face
> On his Repealless – List.
>
> (409)[41]

These young men – thousands of them – will never again be seen on earth and our awareness of God's omniscience does not brighten the bleak landscape.

She had been chilled by 'Frazer's murder'. Now she could identify as never before with the young men slaughtered on battlefields throughout the land:

> My Portion is Defeat – today –
> A paler luck than Victory –
> Less Paeans – fewer Bells –
> The Drums dont follow Me – with tunes –
> Defeat – a somewhat slower – means –
> More Arduous than Balls –
>
> Tis populous with Bone and stain –
> And Men too straight to stoop again,
> And Piles of solid Moan –
> And Chips of Blank – in Boyish Eyes –
> And scraps of Prayer –
> And Death's surprise,
> Stamped visible – in Stone –
>
> There's somewhat prouder, over there –
> The Trumpets tell it to the Air –
> How different Victory

> To Him who has it – and the One
> Who to have had it, would have been
> Contenteder – to die –
>
>   (639)[42]

Her tribute to the defeated builds in intensity through battlefield images both vivid and surprising ('Bone and stain'; 'solid Moan'; 'Chips of Blank'; 'scraps of Prayer'; 'Death's surprise'); it has a grim realism, especially in the second stanza, that sets it far apart from its more famous antebellum predecessor, 'Success is counted sweetest' (67) – a poem that develops a similar theme with more conventional (more literary) battle imagery. A significant difference in the later poem is the direct involvement of the speaker-persona: 'The Drums dont follow Me – with tunes – / Defeat – a somewhat slower – means – / More Arduous than Balls – ' (Her own sense of defeat in Amherst was as great as that of the soldier on the field.) But the most significant difference between this poem and such earlier elegies as 'Bless God, he went as soldiers' (147) is the transformation of celestial apotheosis on the battlefield into 'scraps of Prayer – '[43]

4

During a battle engagement in July of 1863, Higginson was grazed by an exploding shell and severely bruised; and he saw the head of one of his soldiers blown off.[44] At about the same time (though the date cannot be fixed with certainty), Dickinson sent a letter to her Preceptor (L282) enclosing the last half of a poem that vividly recounts a narrow escape with death.[45] Written in about 1861, 'That after Horror – that 'twas *us* – ' has a last stanza chillingly relevant to Higginson's precarious wartime existence:

> That after Horror – that 'twas *us*
> That passed the mouldering Pier –
> Just as the Granite Crumb let go –
> Our Savior, by a Hair –
>
> A second more, had dropped too deep
> For Fisherman to plumb –
> The very profile of the Thought
> Puts Recollection numb –
>
> The possibility – to pass

Without a Moment's Bell –
Into Conjecture's presence –
Is like a Face of Steel –
That suddenly looks into our's
With a metallic grin –
The Cordiality of Death –
Who drills his Welcome in –

(286)[46]

A crumbling ledge high above the water dislodges and falls a moment after Dickinson's persona passes; what might have been (a plunge to a watery death) seizes hold of her consciousness. But the outlines are all that her shocked recollection can bring forth; she cannot reenact the fatal fall – but is instead confronted by death itself, offering diabolical hospitality with 'Face of Steel' and 'metallic grin'. After Jesus has triumphed over the temptations of the devil in the wilderness, he begins to preach; and when he sees two fishermen casting a net into the Sea of Galilee, he says to them: 'Follow me, and I will make you fisher of men' (Matthew 4:1–19). In Dickinson's other poems, the word 'Savior' almost invariably refers to Jesus; here it is the crumbling pier that holds just long enough to save her. If it had not (and it is that 'possibility' that is the overpowering horror), her plunge would have been too deep 'For Fisherman to plumb – ' (and deep enough for satanic Death to drill his welcome in). In the sing-song measure of Watts, Dickinson gives us a powerful new hymn on man who 'knoweth not his time' – one that leaves the cautionary messages of Watts far behind.[47]

'That after Horror – that 'twas *us* – ' has as its subject the precariousness of all human existence; and her text may well have been taken from Ecclesiastes, a book she knew well: 'For man also knoweth not his time: . . . so are the sons of men snared in an evil time, when it falleth suddenly upon them' (9:12). But the message of the Preacher is for us all to remember that 'God shall bring every work into judgment, with every secret thing, whether it be good, or whether it be evil' (12:14). A lesson is not appended to Dickinson's re-creation of a narrow escape; she enters instead into the mind of one who narrowly escapes being 'Snared in an evil time' – and allows the horrifying implications to speak for themselves.

In her penetrating commentary, Sharon Cameron observes that the speaker in this poem struggles unsuccessfully to comprehend and depict the experience of near-death: 'Scrutiny does not expand the experiential instant, cannot pry it apart for more substantial examination.' But the concluding stanza, Cameron suggests, evokes a confrontation that is all too substantial: 'In the last five lines of the poem all the earlier characteristics of the experience suddenly reverse themselves and what was evasive is now inevitable; what vague, now harrowingly delimited.'[48] It was this concluding stanza that Dickinson sent to Higginson in the midst of war. In 'The Procession of the Flowers', he had told of the patches of meadow, marvellously delimited, 'where each flower seems to bloom earliest, without variation, year by year'. Now she stripped away the narrative framework and watery setting so that Higginson could supply his own account of confrontations with death and his own setting. The meadow was now a battlefield.

Another extraordinary poem, written in about 1862, deals in a very different way with the idea of a terrifying plunge. The subject is the precarious survival of a soul – and the final stanza seems to link the persona's private crisis (separation from her beloved) to the horror of a battlefield:

> A Pit – But Heaven over it –
> And Heaven beside, and Heaven abroad;
> And yet a Pit –
> With Heaven over it.
>
> To stir would be to slip –
> To look would be to drop –
> To dream – to sap the Prop
> That holds my chances up.
> Ah! Pit! With Heaven over it!
>
> The depth is all my thought –
> I dare not ask my feet –
> 'Twould start us where we sit
> So straight you'd scarce suspect
> It was a Pit – with fathoms under it
> Its Circuit just the same
> Seed – summer – tomb –
> Whose Doom to whom
>
> 'Twould start them –
> We – could tremble –

> But since we got a Bomb –
> And held it in our Bosom –
> Nay – Hold it – it is calm –
>   (1712)[49]

Here Dickinson evokes the horror of 'The Pit and the Pendulum' –
but in place of shadowy inquisitors and gothic trappings, Dickinson
gives us a victim fully aware of the yawning pit and its terrible
depth. Poe's narrator saves himself while exploring his cell in total
darkness; Dickinson's persona is paralysed by terror, immobilised
between hope and hopelessness. The ironical dilemma of Poe's
narrator (by saving himself he only preserves himself for further
torment) has its counterpart in Dickinson's poem: The bomb in
her bosom (her suffering) threatens her with destruction and, at
the same time, calms her and preserves her from a fatal plunge
into the vast void of permanent hopelessness. Transplanted from
battlefield to bosom, the bomb may be a powerful trope for the
suffering brought on by a war that sent into exile her dearest earthly
friend, the Reverend Dr Charles Wadsworth.[50]

A violent imagery suggestive of suffering (enlarged by the horrors
of the Civil War) is conveyed in 'A Pit – But Heaven over it – ' and
numerous other poems written during this period of national and
personal crisis. Early in the war, she had written to her Norcross
cousins about God's seeming indifference to the suffering she was
witnessing ('. . . The seeing pain one can't relieve makes a demon
of one' [L234]). Later, possibly in 1864, she wrote again to remark
with wonder that Robert Browning could make new poems (his wife
had recently died); but on further thought she understood full well
and reflected on the anguish of the war – and on the enhanced value
of life during these times:

> . . . Sorrow seems more general than it did, and not the estate of
> a few persons, since the war began; and if the anguish of others
> helped one with one's own, now would be many medicines.
>   'Tis dangerous to value, for only the precious can alarm. I
> noticed that Robert Browning had made another poem, and was
> astonished – till I remembered that I, myself, in my smaller way,
> sang off charnel steps. Every day life feels mightier, and what we
> have the power to be, more stupendous. (L298)[51]

She was now singing hundreds of songs 'off charnel steps'.

5

In September 1863, Emily Dickinson became ill – and, beginning in April 1864, went to Boston for extensive treatments for eye troubles; during her seven-month course of treatments, she stayed with her Norcross cousins in nearby Cambridgeport.[52] In response to a letter from Higginson, still convalescing from his war wound, she wrote – from Cambridgeport in June 1864—to express concern about his condition and to tell of her own trouble. She is 'surprised and anxious' since receiving his note, and advises him (through the opening stanza of a poem incorporated into her letter):

> The only News I know
> Is Bulletins all day
> From Immortality.

She asks whether he can make out her pencilled scrawl ('The Physician has taken away my Pen') and tells him, in closing, that 'Knowledge of your recovery – would excel my own – ' (L290). They were both, in a sense, casualties of the war.

Dickinson was forced to return to Boston for additional eye treatments (from April to October 1865); it was not until January 1866— after an eighteen-month lapse in their correspondence – that she wrote again to tell Higginson of the death of her dog Carlo (her 'Shaggy Ally') – and to enclose a poem, 'Further in Summer than the Birds' (L314). She wrote again soon after in response to his desire to see her in Boston ('Is it more far to Amherst?') – and to enclose a clipping of her poem, 'A narrow Fellow in the Grass', from the front page of the *Springfield Republican* for 4 February , published, she assures him, without her authorisation – and and with faulty punctuation ('Lest you meet my Snake and suppose I deceive it was robbed of me – defeated too of the third line by the punctuation').[53] She reminds him of an earlier statement that 'I did not print' (at the beginning of their correspondence she had told him that publication was as 'foreign to my thought, as Firmament to Fin – ' [L265]) – and feared that he might think her 'ostensible' (defined in her lexicon as 'proper or intended to be shown'). She urges him to remain her teacher – and encloses, along with the clipping, her poem 'A Death blow is a Life blow to some' (L316).

Their correspondence revolved, during the next few years, about their shared desire for a meeting. In one of the few of his letters to

Dickinson that have survived, Higginson wrote (in May 1869) to tell her how much her letters and poems both fascinated and baffled him and how elusive she was to him:

> Sometimes I take out your letters & verses, dear friend, and when I feel their strange power, it is not strange that I find it hard to write & that long months pass. I have the greatest desire to see you, always feeling that perhaps if I could once take you by the hand I might be something to you; but till then you only enshroud yourself in this fiery mist & I cannot reach you, but only rejoice in the rare sparkles of light.

He assures her that his interest in her is constant – that he is always the same toward her. He would like to hear from her more often 'but feel always timid lest what I *write* should be badly aimed & miss that fine edge of thought'. He conveys concern about her solitary life so far from the stir of intellectual companionship, but reflects further that 'it isolates one anywhere to . . . have such luminous flashes as come to you – so perhaps the place does not make much difference'. He urges her to come to Boston – and tells her about cultural events that might appeal to her (though his object is, he says, 'to see you, more than to entertain you'). He urges her to tell him more in prose and verse – and he 'will be less fastidious in future & willing to write clumsy things, rather than none' (L330a).

Insufficient attention has been paid to this extraordinary letter and to its implications. Much has been made of the great gulf between the two, of Higginson's inadequacy as a literary critic and as a friend. (His attempts to smooth out her unconventionalities of metre and language were, Thomas H. Johnson has suggested, efforts 'to measure a cube by the rules of [plane] geometry'.)[54] Despite Higginson's obvious limitations, Dickinson had chosen well: He experienced the 'strange power' of her letters and poems, and rejoiced in 'the rare sparkles of light' that came to him; and this was in 1869, long before posthumous recognition and fame. He understood and respected her approach to her sacred vocation – and he responded to her appeals to intercede when, in Higginson's words, 'her verses found too much favor for her comfort, and she was urged to publish'.[55] From her earliest letters to the end of her life, Dickinson conveyed her profound indebtedness to Higginson – and her inability ever to find words adequate to express her deep gratitude; 'To thank you, baffles me' (L268), she said repeatedly all of her life.[56]

Higginson came to Amherst and the much-discussed and anticipated visit finally took place on 16 August 1870; he was greatly
moved by it and recorded his vivid impressions (of two encoun-
ters with the poet) in two long letters to his wife (L342a and
L342b). It was, he informed her, 'a remarkable experience, quite
equalling my expectation'. The poet was, Higginson observed, shy
and childlike in manner, but after some hesitant preliminaries,
free and forthcoming. Higginson was intrigued by and recorded
Dickinson's striking and enigmatic sayings which, he informed his
wife, 'you would have thought foolish & I wise – & some things
you wd. hv. liked'. Among the dozen or so that he transcribed (with
what seems an attentive and accurate ear for Dickinson's distinctive
expression) are these two – the first defining poetry, the second the
way most people live:

> "If I read a book [and] it makes my whole body so cold no fire
> ever can warm me I know *that* is poetry. If I feel physically as if
> the top of my head were taken off, I know *that* is poetry. These
> are the only way I know it. Is there any other way."
>
> "How do most people live without any thoughts. There are
> many people in the world (you must have noticed them in the
> street) How do they live. How do they get strength to put on their
> clothes in the morning[.]"

As an admirer of Thoreau, Higginson could appreciate the Thorea-
uvian trenchancy of her comment on many of the lives she observed
around her – lives without purpose or meaning; but the intense
subjectivity of her definition of poetry clashed with his own rather
genteel approach to literary art – an approach that emphasised
polish and control. ('You think my gait "spasmodic" – I am in
danger – Sir – You think me "uncontrolled" – I have no Tribunal',
she wrote early in their correspondence – in answer to his criticism
of poems she had sent him [L265]).

Higginson's ambivalent response to Dickinson's poems carried
over to the effect the poet herself had on him during their meeting:
'I never was with any one who drained my nerve power so much',
he wrote to his wife; 'Without touching her, she drew from me. I am
glad not to live near her.'[57] Higginson also conveyed to his wife a
terse and revealing portrait of the poet's father: 'I saw Mr. Dickinson
this morning a little – thin dry & speechless – I saw what her life had
been' (L342b). Thirty years later, Higginson recalls the poet's effect

on him in much the same way ('The impression undoubtedly made
on me was that of an excess of tension, and of an abnormal life')
– but he also provides a comment on their meeting that clarifies
Higginson's lifelong importance to her:

> . . . this interview left our relation very much what it was before;
> – on my side an interest that was strong and even affectionate,
> but not based on any thorough comprehension; and on her side
> a hope, always rather baffled, that I should afford some aid in
> solving her abstruse problem of life.

Her abstruse problem of life centered on the question of immortality,
'the Flood subject' that she searchingly examined and reexamined all
of her life.

Higginson's belief in an afterlife – and in the possibility of
communicating with the spirits of the dead – was unquestioning and
unshakable.[58] In contrast, Dickinson's faith in immortality was never
free from profound questioning – though it was always available to
her as a source of strength at a time of crisis. (On occasion, she
provided her strength and solace to Higginson when he experienced
bereavement.) At such times, her questions were set aside and her
profound belief prevailed – a belief all the more profound because
it was constantly being tested.

6

On entering the parlor of the Dickinson house during his first visit,
Higginson noticed among other books copies of his *Out-Door Papers*
and *Malbone: An Oldport Romance* (L342a). About *Out-Door Papers*,
a volume containing five of his *Atlantic* nature essays, Dickinson
wrote to him years later: 'It is still distinct as Paradise – the opening
your first Book – ' (L458); and in another letter, she told him
the lesson of life she had learned from his novel: 'Candor – my
Preceptor – is the only wile. Did you not teach me that yourself,
in the "Prelude" to "Malbone"?' (L450)

In the 'Prelude' to his novel, Higginson observes:

> One learns, in growing older, that no fiction can be so strange
> nor appear so improbable as would the simple truth; and that
> doubtless even Shakespeare did but timidly transcribe a few of
> the deeds and passions he had personally known. For no man
> of middle age can dare trust himself to portray life in its full

intensity, as he has studied or shared it; he must resolutely set aside as indescribable the things most worth describing, and must expect to be charged with exaggeration, even when he tells the rest.[59]

That truth is stranger than fiction is an idea frequently expressed – but the view that even Shakespeare is an inadequate transcriber of man's passions is much less a commonplace. Her vehement response to Higginson's observation on Shakespeare's inadequacy when his portrayal of life is set alongside the deeds and passions of ordinary life may have been occasioned, in part, because she had already said much the same thing – in a bolder and more forceful way: In 'Drama's Vitallest Expression is the Common Day', a poem written about 1863 (discussed in the preceding chapter), Dickinson finds Shakespeare overshadowed by ordinary events ('"Hamlet" to Himself were Hamlet – / Had not Shakespeare wrote – ') – and the most powerful tragedy is that enacted in the human heart ('Only Theatre recorded / Owner cannot shut – ') (741).[60]

Equally meaningful to Dickinson, may have been *Malbone*'s concluding chapter, titled 'Requiescat' – and its account of the heroine's life of patient and courageous renunciation after she has lost her beloved:

Must all novels end with an earthly marriage, and nothing be left for heaven? . . . Were this life all, its very happiness were sadness. If, as I doubt not, there be another sphere, then that which is unfulfilled in this must yet find completion . . . . And though a thousand oracles should pronounce this thought an idle dream, neither Hope nor I would believe them.[61]

Dickinson's poems of earthly renunciation and celestial marriage reach far beyond the stilted sentimentality of Higginson's language and the sunny certitude of his belief – but his unquestioning commitment to his vision of immortality gave strength and comfort to her own restless and endless religious quest.

In the *Scribner's Monthly* for June 1874, Higginson's Memorial Day poem, 'Decoration', pays tribute to the war dead; the speaker in the poem stands in a military cemetery, lilies in hand, and asks his fallen comrades 'in what soldier-grave / Sleeps the bravest of the brave?' Turning from 'the flower-wreath'd tombs' that surround him, Higginson's persona comes to a neglected grave that 'Bears no roses, wears no wreath' – and strews his lilies there to honor this forgotten hero, 'the bravest of the brave'.[62] Higginson's five-stanza poem is a mechanical exercise in versified sentiment ('Yet no heart more high and warm / Ever dared the battle-storm') but it elicited a profound, and profoundly revealing, response from Emily Dickinson. Just about two weeks after the publication of 'Decoration', Edward Dickinson suddenly died – and, in answer to Higginson's message of condolence, the poet wrote to her Preceptor: 'Your beautiful Hymn, was it not prophetic? It has assisted that Pause of Space which I call "Father" – ' (L418)[63]

'His Heart was pure and terrible', she wrote to Higginson in the same letter, 'and I think no other like it exists'; and she adds: 'I am glad there is Immortality – but would have tested it myself – before entrusting him.' In the spring of 1876, she writes again to express pleasure that Higginson liked 'Immortality' (possibly a reference to her poem '"Faithful to the end" Amended') and to reflect on her 'Father's lonely Life and his lonelier Death' – for which, she explains in a brief poem, there is this compensation:

> Take all away –
> The only thing worth larceny
> Is left – the Immortality –
>
> (L457)[64]

Higginson had conveyed his concern, on several occasions, about *her* lonely life and she had emphatically assured him that his concern was unfounded; now she was conveying to Higginson her sense of her father's isolation – not a physical separation but a temperamental rigour and remoteness that cut him off from those around him.[65] (Lavinia is reported to have said of her father, 'he never kissed us goodnight in his life – He would have died for us, but he would have died before he would have let us know it'.)[66]

On what seems to have been the third anniversary of her father's death, Dickinson wrote to Higginson to convey her hope that her Preceptor might come to her again – and to tell of her great sense of loss and change ('Since my Father's dying, everything sacred enlarged so – it was dim to own – ') She recalls attending a funeral when a child and hearing the clergyman's question: 'Is the Arm of the Lord shortened that it cannot save?' His stress on the word *cannot* suggested to her a doubt about immortality that, she says, 'besets me still, though we know that the mind of the Heart must live if it's clerical part do not'. She knows that he was once a clergyman and asks if he has experienced a similar thought ('It comforts an instinct if another have felt it too'). She has been rereading his 'Decoration' and offers to her Preceptor a four-line redaction of his five-stanza tribute to a fallen hero:

> Lay this Laurel on the One
> Too intrinsic for Renown –
> Laurel – vail your deathless tree –
> Him you chasten, that is He!
>
> (L503)

Higginson's lilies are transformed into a wreath offered to one of too great a value to be valued by the many; in the words of the Book of Revelation, he is one who 'may have right to the tree of life' (22:14) – one who has been loved and chastened by the Spirit of God ('As many as I love, I rebuke and chasten' [3:19]). Before the war, she had celebrated the courage of those 'Who charge within the bosom / The Cavalry of Wo – '; now she paid homage to her dead father in a quatrain inspired by Higginson's tribute to a dead soldier, 'the bravest of the brave'. (In his turn, Higginson paid tribute to her poem as vastly superior to his own. While preparing *Poems*, *Second Series*, Higginson copied out 'Lay this Laurel on the One' and informed Mabel Loomis Todd: 'She wrote it after re-reading my "Decoration." It is the combined essence of that & so far finer.')[67]

Several months after sending Higginson her version of his 'Decoration', she wrote again to offer sympathy on the death of his wife, long an invalid. Dickinson was now moved to become *his* Preceptor – and to enclose a quatrain that offered a consoling view of the spirit world that paralleled his own:

> Dear Friend.
>
> If I could help you?
>
>> Perhaps she does not go so far
>> As you who stay – suppose –
>> Perhaps comes closer, for the lapse
>> Of her corporeal clothes –
>
> Did she know she was leaving you? The Wilderness is new – to you. Master, let me lead you.
>
> (L517)

She understood that such a consoling view, however deeply felt, had limited efficacy at such a time and sent another letter soon after to ask about his well-being – and to convey her understanding about the ordeal he was experiencing: 'Do not try to be saved – but let Redemption find you – as it certainly will – Love is it's own rescue, for we – at our supremest, are but it's trembling Emblems – ' (L522)

The widowed Higginson remarried in 1879; 'I heard you had found the Lane to the Indies, Columbus was looking for – ' Dickinson wrote to him on learning of her Preceptor's engagement to Mary Thacher (L575). The author of an elegant volume of nature essays, the new bride – more than twenty years younger than Higginson – was described by him as a shy and modest old-fashioned girl ('no man ever had a sweeter or lovelier angel for a wife & more adapted to his needs', he wrote in his diary) – a characteristic paternalism that helps explain his ambivalent feelings about Emily Dickinson.[68]

Higginson, who loved children, had been disappointed by the childlessness of his first marriage. He and his new wife rejoiced on the arrival of their firstborn child (named Louisa, after his mother); their happiness was shattered when, in March 1880, their seven week-old infant died. Dickinson wrote several messages of sympathy, for the most part profound and elegiac ('These sudden intimacies with Immortality are expanse – not Peace – as Lightning at our feet, instills a foreign Landscape' [L641]). But the communication that most moved Higginson was one that conveys its intimacy with immortality by evoking a vision of life so all-encompassing in its exuberance that it diminishes death. In one of her condolence letters, the poet tells about an American Indian, a woman with a little girl, who came to the Homestead kitchen door to sell baskets. The woman tells her about a young son who has died. Dickinson then escorts the baby, who likes 'to step', into the garden:

> I was touchingly reminded of your little Louisa this Morning by an Indian Woman with gay Baskets and a dazzling Baby, at the Kitchen Door – Her little Boy "once died," she said, Death to her dispelling him – I asked her what the Baby liked, and she said "to step." The Prairie before the Door was gay with Flowers of Hay, and I led her in – She argued with the Birds – she leaned on Clover Walls and they fell, and dropped her – With jargon sweeter than a Bell, she grappled Buttercups – and they sank together, the Buttercups the heaviest – What sweetest use of Days! (L653)

After the poet's death, Higginson chose this letter as the last among the many that he reproduced in his *Atlantic* essay 'Emily Dickinson's

Letters'; but he removed from the opening sentence what would have been an inappropriate identification ('your little Louisa') by substituting a more impersonal reference, in brackets: 'I was touchingly reminded of [a child who had died] . . . .'[69]

In his essay, Higginson suggests that this letter was especially valued because it displayed a greater intimacy of observation and sympathy than was usually shown in her letters. He may also have been struck, as a literary critic who had praised Andrew Marvell's 'vital vigor' (in 'Letter to a Young Contributor'), by an echo from Marvell in Dickinson's letter. In her image of the baby grappling with and falling among flowers, Dickinson seems to be recalling lines from 'The Garden': 'What wondrous life is this I lead! / . . . / Stumbling on melons, as I pass, / Ensnared in flowers, I fall on grass.'[70]

A new child, Margaret, was born to the Higginsons in the summer of 1881—and the poet wrote to express her gladness and her 'hope it may make no farther flight than it's Father's Arms – ' (L728). A measure of Higginson's great personal regard for Dickinson is the strong likelihood that he had confided in her, early in the pregnancy, that his wife was expecting a second child. ('I am tenderly happy that you are happy – Thank you for the Whisper – ' she wrote to him in November 1880, about eight months before Margaret's birth [L675]).[71] When little Gilbert died suddenly, in October 1883, the poet did not inform Higginson about this grievous blow perhaps, in part, out of tactful concern over reopening parental wounds (and arousing parental anxieties). She did, however, share her grief with Higginson in an oblique way.

On the fourth anniversary of the death of baby Louisa (and five months after Gilbert's death), Dickinson sent to Higginson a 'delayed Valentine for your little Girl – '; this was the enclosed message for Margaret Higginson, not yet three years old – a slightly altered version of one of the elegies for Gilbert she had sent across the lawn to Sue:

> In memory of your Little Sister
>   Who "meddled" with the costly Hearts to which she gave the
>   worth and broke them – fearing punishment, she ran away
>   from Earth – (L894 and L893)

Her message and poem told her Preceptor about her awareness of this special day – and about her concern over the painful associations it must have for him and his wife. She had, in the past, shared with him news about her own trials and bereavements. She was tactfully silent about the death of Gilbert – but the poem she sent in memory of the infant Louisa (Gilbert's poem, with pronouns altered) was also a hidden message about her own bereavement.[72]

Fifteen months before her death, Dickinson wrote again to her Preceptor, this time to express pleasure that J. W. Cross's *Life* of George Eliot had finally been published – and that it was now possible for her to send him a copy of the book, a long-promised gift. 'Biography first convinces us of the fleeing of the Biographied – ' she informs Higginson, a wry comment on the difficulty of accepting the reality of the death of one who means much to us; and she adds another of the elegies written after Gilbert's death, the one incorporated into the first of a series of letters to Sue ('The Vision of Immortal Life has been fulfilled – ' [L868]); Gilbert's quatrain now serves to mark the departure of a writer whose novels made her a living presence to Dickinson:

> Pass to thy Rendezvous of Light,
> Pangless except for us –
> Who slowly ford the Mystery
> Which thou has leaped across!
>
> (L972)

The mystery that all of us slowly ford was a perennial subject of interest to her – as it was, she knew, to her Preceptor.

7

The last of her letters to Higginson was (with the exception of the two-word message that she sent to her Norcross cousins before lapsing into the coma that preceded her death) the last letter she ever wrote; it was a ten word message prompted by an item in the *Springfield Republican* about Higginson's cancellation of a lecture because of illness:

> Deity – does He live now?
> My friend – does he breathe?
>
> (L1045)[73]

'She was asking the Unitarian minister the same question about God', observes Anna Mary Wells, 'that she had once asked the literary critic about her work'.[74]

The two questions, separated by twenty-four years of close friendship and a prolific correspondence, are intimately linked. Dickinson's vocation as a poet was a sacred one to her and her flood subject, she told Higginson, was immortality. She was thoroughly attuned to Higginson's message, in 'Letter to a Young Contributor', that fame or oblivion are temporary distinctions of little importance when set alongside the prospect of 'some other realm of existence'. Higginson had resigned his pulpit and had little patience with doctrinal orthodoxy; but his faith in an afterlife was fixed and unwavering. That faith was far more important to Dickinson than any praise he could offer (or withhold) in critical response to the poems she sent him.

The last question that she asked him, in the last days of her life, she had asked before: After her father's death, she asked Higginson – as the clergyman he once was – to clarify for her the questions about immortality that had long troubled her (L503). Unlike Higginson's unorthodox but unswerving faith (discussed in the following chapter), her own faith was rooted in a fierce and restless search for a truth that kept eluding her – a search given strength by those she could admire (like Wadsworth and Higginson) who had found the certainty that kept eluding her. In the presence of death, she came closest to the 'uncertain certainty' that she maintained in uneasy equilibrium throughout her lifetime:

> Of Paradise' existence
> All we know
> Is the uncertain certainty –
> But it's vicinity infer,
> By it's Bisecting
> Messenger –
>
> (1411)

Dickinson's expression of faith in this poem, suggests Peggy Anderson, amplifies the plea to Jesus by a recent convert (whose son has just been miraculously cured): 'I believe; help thou mine unbelief' (Mark 9:24).[75]

During her anguish over little Gilbert's death, Dickinson wrote to tell Elizabeth Holland of the 'Nervous prostration' that the doctors had diagnosed. She does not know what to call it, she informs her friend – but does know that it is a crisis of sorrow over the many she cannot bear to lose that tires her: 'As Emily Bronte to her Maker,

I write to my Lost "Every Existence would exist in thee – "' (L873). Her quotation is from the sixth stanza of Brontë's 'No coward soul is mine' – a poem that was especially meaningful to Dickinson. It was the poem that Higginson would read at Emily Dickinson's funeral on 19 May 1886.

The Reverend George S. Dickerman read a passage from First Corinthians referred to as greatly valued by Dickinson ('For this corruptible must put on incorruption, and this mortal must put on immortality' [15:53]). Higginson, who had come to Amherst for the occasion, spoke briefly and read the poem by Emily Brontë which he described as 'a favorite with our friend who has now put on that Immortality which she seemed never to have laid off'; Higginson's choice was an appropriate one – for Brontë's theme is a version of the message she had sent to him after the death of his wife ('Love is it's own rescue, for we – at our supremest, are but it's trembling Emblems – '), a sacred message central to her life and work:

> No coward soul is mine,
> No trembler in the world's storm-troubled sphere:
> I see Heaven's glories shine,
> And faith shines equal, arming me from fear.
>
> . . . .
>
> Though earth and man were gone,
> And suns and universes ceased to be,
> And thou were left alone,
> Every existence would exist in thee.
>
> There is not room for Death,
> Nor atom that his might could render void:
> Thou – thou art Being and Breath,
> And what thou art may never be destroyed.

A local newspaper account of the funeral refers to Colonel Higginson's reading of 'a strikingly appropriate poem' – and tells how 'The sun was shining in glory, and all the air was sweet with the perfume of blossoming trees, as the mortal part of this gifted woman was laid beside those of her parents'.[76]

Drawing on the medieval motto *astra castra, numen lumen* ('the stars my camp, the Deity my light') Higginson wrote a poem shortly after the poet's death about a woman, a 'freed spirit', who now dwells in some other realm of existence:

ASTRA CASTRA.

Somewhere betwixt me and the farthest star,
   Or else beyond all worlds, all space, all thought,
   Dwells that freed spirit, now transformed and taught
      To move in orbits where the immortals are.
Does she rejoice or mourn? Perchance from far
   Some earthly errand she but now has sought,
   By instantaneous ways among us brought,
      Ways to which night and distance yield no bar.
Could we but reach and touch that wayward will
   On earth so hard to touch, would she be found
   Controlled or yet impetuous, free or bound,
Tameless as ocean, or serene and still?
   If in her heart one eager impulse stirs,
   Could heaven itself calm that wild mood of hers?[77]

The spirit world that Higginson believed in is now the domain of this freed spirit and the speaker in the poem speculates on the possibility of her carrying out some earthly errand from afar – and of our reaching out to one who was so elusive to us on earth. Soon after the publication of 'Astra Castra' in a volume of his poems, Higginson gave the same title to a Dickinson poem and included it, among thirteen others, in a magazine essay announcing the imminent publication of *Poems by Emily Dickinson* (1890); here is 'Departed – to the Judgment – ' (524) as it appeared in the *Christian Union*, with Higginson's title:

ASTRA CASTRA.

Departed to the Judgment!
   A mighty afternoon;
Great clouds, like ushers, leaning,
   Creation looking on.

The flesh surrendered, canceled,
   The bodiless begun;
Two worlds, like audiences disperse,
   And leave the soul alone.[78]

Charles Wadsworth tells, in 'A Spectacle to Angels', how 'Paul represents himself as acting [in a great amphitheatre], while the angelic host look down from their seats as a "great cloud of witnesses"'. Our world, says Wadsworth to his congregation, is a theatre 'whereon men act, as in a drama, "a spectacle to angels"' – until 'this gay drapery of life falls off' and we ascend 'to the higher and trans-sepulchral life, to act nobler parts in the service of the Master . . .'. [79] In his version of 'Astra Castra', Higginson depicts (in the modish voice of poesy ['Perchance from afar / Some earthly errand she but now has sought']) a restless, wandering spirit; Wadsworth's rapturous sermon pictures a surrender of the flesh that enables the liberated spirit to act a nobler part on a greater stage. Dickinson's evocation of landscape and skyscape at the moment of death is a darker vision than that of Higginson or Wadsworth. We are addressed in Common Metre, a cadence that links the cosmic drama being enacted to the immediacy of a singing-speaking voice – a voice that provides us with a chilling glimpse of a solitary soul isolated from both the world of the living and the world of the dead.

'I can't tell you how much I am enjoying the poems', Higginson wrote to Mabel Loomis Todd as they began their labours of compiling a volume for publication; he told of 'many new to me which take my breath away & which also have *form* beyond most of those I have seen before'.[80] The poem 'Departed to the Judgment!' (titled by Higginson 'Astra Castra') seems to have been one of these newly encountered poems that took his breath away. He describes it, in his *Christian Union* essay, 'An Open Portfolio', as 'approaching the great change from time to eternity at a different angle' – and with 'superb concentration'.[81] He found it strong enough to reproduce in this first public display of this private poet – in advance of the appearance of a volume that would include about two hundred of Dickinson's best and most accessible poems (in the judgement of Todd and Higginson).[82]

During Higginson's long relationship with the poet, his frustra-tion and bafflement were accompanied by admiration and awe. While she lived, he introduced her poems to Helen Hunt Jackson and other literary friends; after her death, he played a less reluctant and far more active role than he has been given credit for.[83] In his *Christian Union* essay introducing her to the public, Higginson cited Ruskin's observation ('no beauty of execution can outweigh one grain or fragment of thought') and called her verses 'in most cases like poetry plucked up by the roots; we have them with earth, stones, and dew adhering, and must accept them as they are'.[84] (Higginson and Todd did not accept them as they were but smoothed away colloquialisms and punctuation to make them more acceptable to the readers of their day; Thomas H. Johnson's variorum edition was a giant step forward – but R. W. Franklin has demonstrated that no single edition can possibly permit us to 'accept them as they are'.)[85] After reproducing 'Two Kinsmen' (the title given to 'I died for Beauty – but was scarce'), Higginson paid Dickinson the great compliment of comparing the poem to the work of so authentic and original a genius as William Blake: ' . . . one can no more criticize a faulty rhyme here and there than a defect of drawing in one of Blake's pictures'; he then adds a sentence that seems a variation on a sentiment that she had conveyed to him during his 1870 visit to the Homestead: 'When a thought takes one's breath away [wrote Higginson in the *Christian Union* in 1890], who cares to count the syllables?'[86] One of the striking sayings that the analytical and observant Higginson had recorded and reported to his wife two decades earlier seems to have struck home: "If I feel physically as if the top of my head were taken off [said Dickinson in 1870] I know *that* is poetry . . . . Is there any other way?"(L342b) She had chosen well when she chose Higginson as her Preceptor. And he learned well from *his* preceptor.

4

Nature's Haunted House: 'Called Back'

'Nature is a Haunted House – but Art – a House that tries to be haunted', the poet wrote to Higginson in 1876 (L459a). As mentioned earlier, she had informed her Preceptor that 'the "supernatural," was only the Natural, disclosed – '; that 'Not "Revelation" – 'tis – that waits, / but our unfurnished eyes – ' (L280) An intense awareness of the relationship between the supernatural and the natural pervades Dickinson's poetry. She found in Higginson a sympathetic friend and a kindred spirit; he was her Preceptor – and he was also an ardent advocate of Christian Spiritualism, a movement that swept America and England in the middle decades of the nineteenth century. In 1853 Nathaniel Parker Willis claimed that there were forty thousand believers in New York alone and the widespread anguish that accompanied the carnage of the war spurred its popularity; in 1867 Emma Hardinge Britten announced that one-fourth of the population of the United States had adopted spiritualism as their creed.[1] However exaggerated this estimate, the spiritualist movement could identify many distinguished writers among its ranks – and Thomas Wentworth Higginson was an influential presence among them.[2]

Higginson lectured and wrote extensively on spiritualism; Wadsworth's views on the afterlife took spiritualist doctrine into account; Edward Hitchcock, Professor of Natural Theology and Geology at Amherst College (after serving as College President for a decade), saw natural science as a great illustrator of the truth of religion – a position that closely paralleled the claims of spiritualism. In addition to Higginson, other literary figures admired by Dickinson were, in different ways, deeply involved with spiritualism – Hawthorne, Elizabeth Barrett Browning and Ruskin among them. For Dickinson, expressions of doubt and despair alternated with (and sometimes accompanied) proclamations of faith; though she could not accept this new doctrine (or any doctrine), her religious quest was carried on in the climate of a burgeoning spiritualist movement that left its mark on her mind and art.

1

In April 1852, when Higginson was invited to head the new Free Church in Worcester, he attended a spiritual séance in Boston to consult with his dead father and brother (lost at sea when Higginson was eighteen) before making his decision; his dead brother was inaccessible but his father's spirit responded to the medium's summons – and urged him on to Worcester. Higginson accepted the call, encouraged also by a more palpable Theodore Parker.[3] Five years later, Higginson submitted a sworn affidavit attesting to the authenticity of supernatural phenomena he had personally witnessed during two séances conducted by a Harvard divinity student suspended for his activities as a spiritualistic medium.[4]

In 'The Results of Spiritualism', a lecture delivered in New York in 1859, Higginson attacked orthodox Christian doctrine for replacing a universal and instinctively felt faith in immortality and an awareness of the never-ending relation between 'the other world and this' with dogma concerning 'a gloomy sleep of ages and an incredible resurrection to end it'. The result was fear of death and loss of hope:

> How do we treat death? With mourning chiefly, with lamentation mainly, not for ourselves alone but for those who have gone forward to a new existence. That which we call death the angels call birth, as that we call sunset is but a radiant sunrise to those farther on beneath the golden West. But how rarely is this admitted in daily life?[5]

God's eternal laws operate so as to free us from fear of death: It is the survivors, not the dying, who are afflicted by fear. Higginson identifies himself as one of those fortunate beings to whom was given by nature a faith in immortality so strong that 'the gloom of theology' could not overcome it. He rejoices in witnessing the beginnings of a movement that is bringing solace to so many sufferers: The joy spiritualism and spiritualists are spreading is a triumph unequalled in the history of the world.[6]

Immortality, for Higginson, meant endless progress: 'That which
we have been sent into the universe to do will be done somewhere.'
He has never been afraid of annihilation or hell – but has trembled
at the thought of a theological heaven exclusively devoted to vocal
music. God has given us work to do – and, most important, a
purpose to carry it forward beyond the grave: 'The course of man
is to be upward, God has put the power into us, and God is true
though every theologian in the world is a liar.'[7]

In 'Safe in their Alabaster Chambers', Dickinson seems to be
joining Higginson in poking fun at the orthodox belief in 'a gloomy
sleep of ages and an incredible resurrection to end it':

> Safe in their Alabaster Chambers –
> Untouched by Morning –
> And untouched by Noon –
> Lie the meek members of the Resurrection –
> Rafter of Satin – and Roof of Stone!
>
> Grand go the Years – in the Crescent – above them –
> Worlds scoop their Arcs –
> And Firmaments – row –
> Diadems – drop – and Doges – surrender –
> Soundless as dots – on a Disc of Snow –
>
> (216, version of 1861)[8]

Dickinson enclosed a copy of this version of the poem in her first
letter to Higginson – and Barton Levi St Armand has suggested
that to him the poem must have resembled the plethora of morbid
graveyard verse sprinkled among the popular gift books of the time;
Jane Donahue Eberwein seems to me to be closer to the mark when
she points out that this is an 'appalling version' – that the poet, in
the opening stanza, 'presents these Christians who have been saved
as "Safe" in imagery suggestive more of a bank deposit vault than
of anything holy'.[9] Higginson seems also closer to the mark when
he prints the second stanza of the 1861 version in his *Christian
Union* essay and pays tribute to its power ('with all its too daring
concentration, it strikes a note too fine to be lost').[10] It is indeed an
extraordinary stanza in which, in twenty-nine words, Dickinson sets
the sleeping dead against a vast backdrop of cycling galaxies and
crumbling empires.

Higginson's playful despair at the thought of a theological heaven
in which 'one's entire existence [is devoted] to vocal music only'

seems to find its playful counterpart in a poem by Dickinson depicting heaven as a never-ending and never-changing Sunday School paradise (while also conveying her disquietude with life on earth):

> I never felt at Home – Below –
> And in the Handsome Skies
> I shall not feel at Home – I know –
> I dont like Paradise –
>
> Because it's Sunday – all the time –
> And Recess – never comes –
> And Eden'll be so lonesome
> Bright Wednesday Afternoons –
>
> (413, stanzas 1 and 2)[11]

Through her child persona, Dickinson deflates this infinitely boring heaven in much the same way Mark Twain, through Huck Finn, would respond to Miss Watson's good place where 'all a body would have to do there was to go around all day long with a harp and sing, forever and ever'.[12] Huck's version of heaven was anticipated two decades earlier by Higginson – and by Dickinson.

Though his faith was firm, Higginson did not attempt to envision the particularities of an afterlife. 'We are not sent into the world to do a certain work', he observed, 'but to lead a noble life'. Whatever our chosen labors on earth, 'great or small they are all little in an eternity, and it is the purpose that makes them great or small'. Those who revere their own lives – and the lives of others – will be called after death 'to something more important'. A man's life on this earth must necessarily be transformed and enlarged by the knowledge that his career is infinite, not finite – by the knowledge that his beloved dead are 'with clearer eyes watching him from the eternal world'.[13] In another of her early poems about heaven, Dickinson's child persona speculates about a paradise that seems a mirror image of a familiar village world:

> What is – "Paradise" –
> Who live there –
> Are they "Farmers" –
> Do they "hoe" –
> Do they know that this is "Amherst" –
> And that I – am coming – too –
>
> (215, stanza 1)

Here again, Dickinson's parodic version of an earthbound paradise (as seen by a child) seems to anticipate the sentimental vision of heaven in Elizabeth Stuart Phelps's *The Gates Ajar* (1868) – and Mark Twain's scornful response to the novel and its 'mean little ten cent heaven about the size of Rhode Island'.[14] The celestial 'Farmers' who 'hoe' in 'Amherst' envisioned by Dickinson's child persona burlesque the kind of earthbound heaven (a deathless prolongation of life on earth) that Higginson rejects in *The Results of Spiritualism*: In that lecture, he asserts that man was created for loftier purposes; that life 'does not end here, it begins here'; that 'Life is the bud, death the opening. . . . '[15] On the occasion of the unveiling of the John Harvard statue in Harvard Yard in April 1884, Dickinson wrote to sculptor Daniel Chester French: 'Success is dust, but an aim forever touched with dew. God keep you fundamental!' (L898).[16] The acclaim that has come to the sculptor is as nothing; the noble aim that led to the creation of the statue is everything – and brings us closer, she seems to imply, to fulfillment in some future unveiling.

Thomas Wentworth Higginson had personally experienced what he believed to be manifestations of the spirits of the dead. In his lecture on spiritualism, he observed that any human being, 'once convinced that he has ever conversed with a departed friend', will be granted the rarest of gifts, the 'joy and peace in believing'. It is enough to revolutionise the world of religious sects, he says, that spirits in another realm of existence 'can have intercourse, however meagre and scanty, with spirits on earth . . . . '[17] For Dickinson, the dead are perpetually beyond the reach of the living – but they are also, she suggests in an undated prose fragment, irresistible 'Lures':

> We do not think enough of the Dead as exhilirants – they are not dissuaders but Lures – Keepers of that great Romance still to us foreclosed – while coveting (we envy) their wisdom we lament their silence. Grace is still a secret. That they have existed none can take away. That they still exist is a trust so daring we thank thee that thou hast hid these things from us and hast revealed them to them. The power and the glory are the post mortuary gifts. (PF 50)

The living cannot know the great secret of the dead and for this Dickinson is grateful. What is also strongly conveyed, however, is that there *is* a great secret, a 'great Romance *still* to us foreclosed – ' (emphasis added). Nothing can be known with certainty in this life – and the power and glory after death is a cherished prospect unknowable on this side of the grave.

The sudden disappearance of those we know from the world of the living was the occasion for a meditation, written in about 1861, on 'the great Romance still to us foreclosed':

> How noteless Men, and Pleiads, stand,
> Until a sudden sky
> Reveals the fact that One is rapt
> Forever from the Eye –
>
> Members of the Invisible,
> Existing, while we stare,
> In Leagueless Opportunity,
> O'ertakeless, as the Air –
>
> Why did'nt we detain Them?
> The Heavens with a smile,
> Sweep by our disappointed Heads
> Without a syllable –
>
> (282)[18]

The opening stanza tells of our tendency to overlook a person and a star until they disappear. Dickinson was acquainted with the legend that all seven of the Pleiades were once visible to the naked eye – that one disappeared from view in ancient times; her lexicon defines *rapt* as 'Transported' – the passive participle of *rap*, 'to snatch or hurry away'. In the poem the hovering cosmic presence of the invisible dead is suggested; but the dead are inaccessible to us ('O'ertakeless, as the Air – ') and the heavens are silently indifferent to, even disdainful of, our influence.

At times, Dickinson explored aspects of the afterworld in ways that paralleled and reinforced Higginson's beliefs; at other times, questioning and doubt prevailed; at all times, his friendship and unwavering faith were a source of great comfort and strength. Her greatest strength was her unwavering dedication to her art – to the dramatisation in her poems of her endless quest and richly varied, sometimes conflicting findings.

2

The Reverend Charles Beecher at first found the rising spiritualist movement a 'subtle but genuine materialism' – a threat to Biblical authority and the church; he later changed his viewpoint and joined with his sister Harriet Beecher Stowe in ardent advocacy of this great new cause.[19] Charles Wadsworth responded to the challenge of spiritualism with an extraordinary sermon, 'The Mortal Immortalized'. Taking as his text 'This mortal must put on immortality' (1 Corinthians 15:53), Wadsworth seeks to correct false impressions of man's condition after death – and comes to conclusions that are not unlike those of Higginson.

In his sermon, Wadsworth identifies two distinct and antagonistic views, '*the Sensuous* and *the Spiritual*', and finds both 'unphilosophic and unscriptural'. The first maintains that personal identity is not at all affected by death and envisions heaven as 'only a glorified earth – immortality only the state of the well-developed mortal!' The second view sees heaven as a state 'utterly unlike all that the mortal has seen and experienced' – one in which the soul, 'in conditions altogether etherealized', survives as a risen spirit rather than as a redeemed man.[20]

The Scriptural text, Wadsworth argues, predicts that man will retain his personal identity – that he will preserve forever, in a transfigured state, all his bodily and mental faculties and functions. The great intellectual works of mortal man ('Milton's song' and 'Newton's march through the universe') will seem like child's play to the mortal mind that puts on immortality.[21] But most important of all will be the transfiguration of 'the heart':

Pure intellect, unsoftened by affection, is simply monstrous. Entering heaven with our logic intensified and our love gone, our sympathies would be fiendish. Affection is, even metaphysically considered, man's noblest attribute. And the more you equip him for the higher spheres of pure intellect, the more fearful and phantom-like you make him, if his ascent is to be out of the power and memory of these beautiful affections of the earthly home and heart.[22]

Transfigured man will enter heaven (retaining the same name he bears on earth) and experience, in social circles gloriously transformed, a perfect love that binds heart to heart with deathless ties ('And it will be a rapturous experience that baptism of the human *heart* with the living water – that induement of these mortal loves with the pomp of immortality').[23]

Though he deplored the widespread view of heaven as 'only a glorified earth', Wadsworth rejected with equal vigour the impersonal and abstract afterworld of orthodoxy: In 'A Spectacle to Angels', the minister vividly evoked a world in which heavenly messengers hover about us as we transact the ordinary and sometimes trivial business of everyday life.[24] When Philadelphia was the host of the great International Centennial Exposition in 1876, Wadsworth preached a sermon, 'Strangers in the Earth', that took as its text Abraham's mournful pronouncement after Sarah's death: 'I am a stranger and a sojourner with you' (Genesis 23:4). The city is filled with 'strangers and sojourners', temporary visitors from every corner of the earth – and the Exposition, he observes, is itself 'a parable God is speaking to us' that we should take to heart. These foreigners, far from home, think tenderly of their native lands – and are models for us all. Good as this Christian life may be, 'Yet there are better things in heaven'. On this earth, we are all strangers and sojourners who need to remember that 'we have a better dwelling-place, and indeed our only true Home, in Heaven – that our great Father . . . is fast gathering into it all our beloved ones, and will presently call us to go up and abide there forever'.[25]

In numerous poems, Dickinson draws on (and transforms and occasionally subverts) these visions of heaven – and heavenly reunion. In one, her persona toys with the idea of ascending to heaven with the face and name of her beloved – still another variation on the exchange of bodies playfully envisioned in the third Master letter (' . . . if I had the Beard on my cheek – like you – and you – had Daisy's petals – and you cared so for me – what would become of you?' [ML, 40]); and she is also playfully translating the message of the Book of Revelation 22:5 ('And they shall see his face; and his name shall be in their foreheads'):

> The face I carry with me – last –
> When I go out of Time –
> To take my Rank – by – in the West –
> That face – will just be thine –
>
> I'll hand it to the Angel –
> That – Sir – Was my Degree -
> In Kingdoms – you have heard the Raised –
> Refer to – possibly.
>
> He'll take it – scan it – step aside –

> Return – with such a crown
> As Gabriel – never capered at –
> And beg me put it on –
>
> And then – he'll turn me round and round –
> To an admiring sky –
> As one that bore her Master's name –
> Sufficient Royalty!
>
> (336)[26]

Such a scene would find a fitting place in Wadsworth's vision of 'God's great universe' as 'only one great family mansion . . .'; such a reunion would not seem blasphemous to a minister who believed that 'unto [man's] *heart* rather than to his *head* shall be accorded the loftiest prizes of eternity!'[27] And such a scene would not seem blasphemous to a minister who gave such a high priority to the divine workings of the human heart – and who was praised for his satiric wit and for his freedom from narrow sectarianism.[28]

In another poem, Dickinson envisions lovers who reach beyond this earth to a rebirth and reunion in heaven:

> 'Twas a long Parting – but the time
> For Interview – had Come –
> Before the Judgment Seat of God –
> The last – and second time
>
> These Fleshless Lovers met –
> A Heaven in a Gaze –
> A Heaven of Heavens – the Privilege
> Of one another's Eyes –
>
> No Lifetime set – on Them –
> Appareled as the new
> Unborn – except They had beheld –
> Born infiniter – now –
>
> Was Bridal – e'er like This?
> A Paradise – the Host –
> And Cherubim – and Seraphim –
> The unobtrusive Guest –
>
> (625)[29]

There is a vivid and witty compression in the sequence of images deployed ('long Parting'; 'last – and second'; 'Fleshless Lovers';

'Heaven in a Gaze') that is far removed from the numerous celestial reunions of her sentimental contemporaries. Dickinson's stanzas are far closer to the stark vision of Vaughan (who saw 'through all this fleshly dresse / Bright shootes of everlastingnesse') – and to the startlingly concrete vision of the Resurrection in Herbert's 'Death' ('When souls shall wear their new array, / And all thy bones with beautie shall be clad').[30]

3

In late July 1849, during the dark hours he experienced while sitting at his dying mother's bedside, Nathaniel Hawthorne came to a bright vision of life after death – a vision he recorded in his journal with startling vehemence:

> Oh what a mockery, if what I saw were all, – let the interval between extreme youth and dying age be filled up with what happiness it might! But God would not have made the close so dark and wretched, if there were nothing beyond; for then it would have been a fiend that created us, and measured out our existence, and not God. It would be something beyond wrong – it would be insult – to be thrust out of life into annihilation in this miserable way. So, out of the very bitterness of death, I gather the sweet assurance of a better state of being.[31]

Sixteen years later, in an address delivered at the funeral of General George Wright at Calvary Church, Charles Wadsworth echoes and amplifies Hawthorne's view of death. After reviewing the general's vigorous life and magnificent achievement, the minister meditates on the lifeless remains. Is this all, he asks: A brief ceremonial tribute 'and then the saddening lot of all carnal things – death's cold, pitiless, starless, terrible oblivion'? If this be all, says Wadsworth, 'then life is at best a mockery'. The testimony of nature refutes so dark a view ('Though this strong man's arm is palsied, yet the imperial spirit that nerved it for the battle is a conqueror still'); and the testimony of the Bible further consoles us with the knowledge that 'death is an eternal "appointment" – . . . An appointment of the omniscience that makes no mistakes; of the beneficence that can work no unkindness'.[32] Neither Hawthorne nor Dickinson could accept this consoling faith in divine omniscience and beneficence, but both were drawn toward it – and dramatised their questionings in their writings.

In 'Insincere Unbelief', Wadsworth addressed the great and difficult question of individual resurrection: How may we hope to be reunited with a loved one who may have died and been buried in a remote part of the globe, whose body may have been destroyed by fire. But is it any more difficult to believe in such a resurrection, the minister asks, than in the creation of the human race and the universe it inhabits:

> I look around, and lo! ten thousand marvelous organisms are filling the landscape with exulting life! I lift my eye to the firmament, and behold! its immensity is crowded with stupendous architecture! And whose are all these wonderful works? Who peopled all these fields of space? Who kindled these great fires of the firmament? Why, God – God! And can this God then be baffled and over-matched by this marvel of the Resurrection?

The answer is a resounding 'no' – and to accept this marvelous manifestation of God's wisdom and power is rational and logical, for 'It is only another marvel amid the great universe of marvels that surround us and press upon us'.[33]

In the Book of Job (32:1–3), Elihu's wrath is directed both against Job (for not accepting God's will) and against the Friends (for condemning Job without answering his complaints); the need to meditate on nature's manifestations in order to open the mind to God's greatness is one of Elihu's affirmations in his exhortation to the suffering Job.[34] Wadsworth draws on Elihu's exhortation in two powerful sermons that dwell on nature's message to suffering mankind.

Wadsworth's text for his sermon 'Songs in the Night' is Elihu's explanation to Job as to why those who are oppressed are not given relief by God: 'None sayeth where is God my maker, who giveth songs in the night' (35:10). 'Night', says Wadsworth, symbolises affliction, 'song' gladness – and 'to say that "God gives songs in the night" is simply to say, God comforts in affliction'. Job's prophetic vision of 'the Redeemer, who was to stand upon the earth' points the way toward men freeing themselves of sin and looking toward immortality – and to a God of consolation, not wrath. 'God comes as an Almighty Comforter into this benighted world, and yet the night is not removed'. The chill and gloom of the air and landscape remain; our afflictions are not removed – but God 'gives us grace to bear it in triumph'.[35]

Wadsworth takes up the part of Elihu's argument that vindicates God's mysterious providences in a sermon, 'The Bright Side'; its text is Elihu's pronouncement: 'Men see not the bright light which is in the cloud' (37:21). Job was engulfed by 'a cloud black as night' – but to his transfigured spirit, Wadsworth observes, the brightness of heaven penetrated the darkness. We are, all of us, enshrouded by dark clouds and the darkest of clouds is death, God's curse upon sin. But even before the blight of sin and death, the first day after the Creation ended in darkness and night; Wadsworth envisions what that scene must have been for the young immortal man in Paradise: 'The sun sinks along the western sky. The shadows lengthen and deepen on the landscape. And then gathers a chill, a gloom, a thick darkness on all things beautiful'. To the eye of faith, shadows are blessed things – and clouds are 'but the curtains God gathers around the blinding splendors of His throne'. Heaven is not far but very near to us; eternity is all around us:

> Just behind this cloud-veil of things, seen and temporal. And see! See how this curtain seems to stir – to tremble, as if the risen and beloved Dead were breathing behind it; as if invisible hands were even now lifting it – parting it. And there!there!is your prepared place – your white robe and sceptre and diadem.[36]

Dickinson could not accept Charles Wadsworth's vision of a heaven reserved for redeemed sinners, could not share his certitude about the afterworld; she was nonetheless responsive to his message – and she shaped it to her own ends as she searched for the truth in her own way.

In several poems, she dramatised our experience of an afterworld in this world, of the fleeting glimpses that are given us from behind the trembling curtain that separates us from the world of the dead. In one of her most haunting lyrics, Dickinson tells of a quality of winter light that seems to come to us from that other world:

> There's a certain Slant of light,
> Winter Afternoons –
> That oppresses, like the Heft
> Of Cathedral Tunes –
>
> Heavenly Hurt, it gives us –
> We can find no scar,

> But internal difference,
> Where the Meanings, are –
>
> None may teach it – Any –
> 'Tis the Seal Despair –
> An imperial affliction
> Sent us of the Air –
>
> When it comes, the Landscape listens –
> Shadows – hold their breath –
> When it goes, 'tis like the Distance
> On the look of Death –
>
> (258)[37]

Winter afternoons are brief and remind us that life is brief and that night (and the night of death) is near. The light is not described; its effect on us – and on the landscape – is described in the language of church rite and sacramental suffering. It is an unearthly light that brings not knowledge but change, 'internal difference', the altered state that follows a religious experience. Hymn book measures (ranging irregularly from *Sevens and Fives* to *Eights and Fives*) are especially apt in a poem that compares the oppressiveness of the light to 'the Heft / of Cathedral Tunes – '; a poem that evokes in 'the Seal Despair' and 'imperial affliction' an apocalyptic vision from one of her favorite Books of the Bible, Revelation: Saint John the Divine beholds, when the fourth seal is opened, a pale horse and a rider named Death (6:7–8).

In 'Tell all the Truth but tell it slant – ' Dickinson's persona observes that 'The Truth must dazzle gradually / Or every man be blind – ' (1129). The dark side of clouds is presented to us on earth, says Wadsworth in 'The Bright Side', 'lest we should be dazed and blinded by the bright splendor of heaven'.[38] A glorious truth is revealed in Wadsworth's sermon and the closing mood is jubilant. In 'There's a certain Slant of light', a mystery is experienced and the closing mood is muffled and oppressive. This slant of penetrating wintry light has told its oblique truth – a dark truth far removed from Wadsworth's bright affirmation but closely attuned to his faith in our proximity to the other world.

4

In *Modern Painters* (1856), Ruskin cites Scripture (1 Corinthians 8:2) to demonstrate the importance of Turner's truthful delineations of nature's infinite mystery:

> Observe, in the first place, this great fact. You never see anything Plainly. It is with sight as with knowledge. It is written: 'If any man think that he knoweth anything, he knoweth nothing yet as he ought to know.' And in the same sense: if any man think that he seeth, he seeth nothing yet as he ought to see. Whatever we look at is full of mystery.[39]

Turner conveyed this mystery by a masterful dance of light in his landscapes – a palpitating light that animates stone, leaf, cloud, wave – 'glowing, or flashing, or scintillating, according to what it strikes; or, in its holier moods, absorbing and enfolding all things in the deep fulness of its repose, and then again losing itself in bewilderment, and doubt, and dimness . . . '.[40] With the passage of years, Ruskin's apocalyptic vision grew darker. (His horror at the fratricidal carnage of the American Civil War contributed to his darkening mood.)[41] He reflected, in 1868, on how any true perception of human life must take into account its vanity and transiency: ' . . . its avenues are wreathed in darkness, and its forms and courses no less fantastic, than spectral; so that . . . it is true of this cloudy life of ours, that "man walketh in a vain shadow, and disquieteth himself in vain."'[42] This bleak vision was accompanied by an awareness of new and ominous cloud formations and strange winds:

> Not rain-cloud, but a dry black veil, which no ray of sunshine can pierce . . . . And everywhere the leaves of the trees are shaking to show the passing to and fro of a strange, bitter, blighting wind . . . . It looks partly as if it were made of poisonous smoke . . . . But mere smoke would not blow to and fro in that wild way. It looks to me as if it were made of dead men's souls.[43]

When, in April 1862, Dickinson told Higginson about the prose writers she admired, her list was short: 'For Prose – Mr Ruskin – Sir Thomas Browne – and the Revelations – ' (L261). Ruskin's haunted visions of mankind and nature, bright and dark, stirred Dickinson profoundly – and she coupled his name with what were to her two great sources of sacred profundity.

For both Ruskin and Dickinson, Barton Levi St Armand observes,

'The landscape always remains mysterious, it is always a "Haunted House," and the artist's corresponding duty is to seek out the hidden ghost and invest his own art with the secret spirit or character of a physical scene'.[44] The enormous difficulty of unraveling that mystery is dramatised in Dickinson's meditation on water, 'What mystery pervades a well!':

> But nature is a stranger yet;
> The ones that cite her most
> Have never passed her haunted house,
> Nor simplified her ghost.
>
> To pity those that know her not
> Is helped by the regret
> That those who know her, know her less
> The nearer her they get.
>
> (1400, stanzas 5 and 6)

The mystery and portentousness of Nature's 'haunted house' are conveyed in numerous poems: 'There's a certain Slant of light' (258); 'Of Bronze – and Blaze – ' (290); 'The Wind begun to knead the Grass' (824); 'The Lightning is a yellow Fork' (1173); 'The Symptom of the Gale – ' (1324); 'There came a Wind like a Bugle – ' (1593), among others.

In 'Of Bronze – and Blaze – ' the incredible grandeur of the northern lights seems the manifestation of a phenomenon outside of nature. Dickinson's persona is moved, by the sky's spectacular display, to majestic posturing alien to her simple nature – and moved finally to a sense of abject insignificance:

> Of Bronze – and Blaze –
> The North – Tonight –
> So adequate – it forms –
> So preconcerted with itself –
> So distant – to alarms –
> An Unconcern so sovreign
> To Universe, or me –
> Infects my simple spirit
> With Taints of Majesty –
> Till I take vaster attitudes –
> And strut upon my stem –
> Disdaining Men, and Oxygen,
> For Arrogance of them –

> My Splendors, are Menagerie –
> But their Competeless Show
> Will entertain the Centuries
> When I, am long ago,
> An Island in dishonored Grass –
> Whom none but Beetles – know.
>   (290)[45]

The unfathomable remoteness and authoritativeness of this heavenly display (removed both from humankind and the universe)
seduces her 'simple spirit' to two kinds of absurd posturing: In
stanza one she struts arrogantly; in stanza two she bemoans the transience of her 'Splendors' (likened to the traveling animal shows that
visited Amherst each year) alongside the 'Competeless Show' of the
northern skies – and envisions (with an exaggerated self-pity that is
a counterpart of the arrogant posturing in stanza one) her neglected
grave centuries hence, unknown to all but beetles.[46] The ironic
posturings of Dickinson's persona underscore a serious purpose:
In the words of Greg Johnson, the poem 'may serve as the paradigm
for Dickinson's awareness of natural process in contrast to her own
mortality'.[47] It is noteworthy that 'natural process' in 'Of Bronze –
and Blaze – ' reaches beyond the natural universe into a mysterious
region that seems not far distant from what Wadsworth called 'The
Bright Side' and Higginson 'some other realm of existence'.

Higginson's celebrations of nature in his *Atlantic* essays are, occasionally, similarly tempered by an awareness of the remoteness of
nature – of man's limited capacity to absorb and appreciate its
infinite splendour and mystery. In 'Snow', for example, he describes
the dazzling tints of a sunny day after a snowstorm – and tells of
'That sensation we poor mortals often have, of being just on the edge
of infinite beauty, yet with always a lingering film between . . . ' .[48]
In another *Atlantic* essay, 'A Shadow', Higginson tells of a solitary
walk in winter on the outskirts of the town while the setting sun
leaves 'a trail of orange light along the horizon' and the lustrous
early stars come into view. These are awesome sights – and the
walker finds himself drawn toward a more earthly, human sight:
The gleam of a window and the shadowy outlines (from behind a
curtain) of a mother and her child.[49] ('I thought I spoke to you of
the shadow – [Dickinson wrote to him soon after its publication] It
affects me – ' [L353]).

On occasion, for Higginson and Dickinson, nature would stop

being remote, would come all too close to man's world – with violent and unpredictable results. In his *Atlantic* 'ghost' story, 'The Haunted Window' (1867), Higginson's narrator and his friend, Severance, are spending a summer together at the sea in Oldport. Severance is obsessed by 'Rutherford's strange old book on the Second Sight' – and by the visitations of what seems an apparition in the window of an old empty house. The narrator also sees a mysterious figure and his friend recites to him the motto of a chapter from the old book that fascinates him:

> "In sunlight one,
> In shadow none,
> In moonlight two,
> In thunder two,
> Then comes Death."

These ominous events are interrupted when the narrator is called away to Boston; on his return, he is witness to a spectacular display in the sky, a sunset likened to a deadly battlefield:

> Returning thence by the stage-coach, we drove from Tiverton, the whole length of the island, under one of those wonderful skies which give, better than anything in nature, the effect of a field of battle. The heavens were filled with ten thousand separate masses of cloud, varying in shade from palest gray to iron-black, borne rapidly to and fro by upper and lower currents of opposing wind. They seemed to be charging, retreating, breaking, recombining, with puffs of what seemed smoke, and a few wan sunbeams sometimes striking through for fire. Wherever the eye turned, there appeared some flying fragment not seen before; and yet in an hour this noiseless Antietam grew still, and a settled leaden film overspread the sky, yielding only to some level lines of light where the sun went down.

Soon after, the thunderstorm erupts and, in the midst of the tumult, the narrator arrives in Oldport – and begins a search for his friend, unaccountably missing. Severance is finally found, fatally injured under a fallen tree.[50]

As St Armand has pointed out, Ruskin's word-painting contributes significantly to Higginson's ominously spectacular sunset in 'The Haunted Window'.[51] (There is an explicit reference to Ruskin's approach to colour in another of Higginson's Oldport sketches, 'In a Wherry'.)[52] The story's ghostly atmosphere and teasingly ironic narrative stance is also greatly indebted to Hawthorne, whose tales and romances he greatly admired: The seeming apparitions are explained by Severance's secret romance – and by the cloaked disguises of a spurned Portugese girl; to the narrator, these events 'seemed like a dream' – and its moral, such as it is, is 'that shadow and substance are always ready to link themselves, in unexpected ways, against the diseased imagination . . . .'[53]

A climactic moment in Higginson's Hawthornesque tale takes place when Severance, trapped beneath a tree, is made aware of the presence of the girl he has abandoned by a lightning flash: 'Gleaming lustrous beneath the lightning', her face expresses her pitying forgiveness to the dying man ('it had a more mystic look when the long flash had ceased, and the single lantern burned before it, like an altar-lamp before a shrine').[54] It is a sanctifying lightning bolt that brings both death and reconciliation.

Jane Donahue Eberwein has summarised the ways in which that awesome phenomenon, lightning – with its combination of illumination and danger – took powerful hold of Dickinson's imagination in numerous poems.[55] In one of them, written during the war, the way in which danger intensifies our awareness of immortality is likened to the sudden materialisation of invisible terrain in the split-second following a lightning flash:

> The Soul's distinct connection
> With immortality
> Is best disclosed by Danger
> Or quick Calamity –
>
> As Lightning on a Landscape
> Exhibits Sheets of Place –
> Not yet suspected – but for Flash –
> And Click – and Suddenness –
> (974)[56]

Dickinson's imagery parallels that of Wadsworth's comment, in his sermon 'Shining Lights', on the fitful and intermittent quality of man's piety – and on how 'at long intervals and on great occasions it may flash and roar like a fearful thunderbolt, and flood the whole landscape with an awful splendor . . . .'[57] Dickinson returned to the lightning imagery of 'The Soul's distinct connection' (and of

Wadsworth's sermon) after the death of Higginson's infant daughter: 'These sudden intimacies with Immortality [she wrote to her friend], are expanse – not Peace – as Lightning at our feet, instills a foreign Landscape' (L641). Sudden danger and death could be, for Dickinson, both menacing and enlarging.

In a late poem, one of her most vivid, an imminent thunderstorm becomes an ominous presence and, when it finally breaks upon them, the people of the village witness a wild dance of the natural elements as they occupy and transform the town:

> There came a Wind like a Bugle –
> It quivered through the Grass
> And a Green Chill upon the Heat
> So ominous did pass
> We barred the Windows and the Doors
> As from an Emerald Ghost –
> The Doom's electric Moccasin
> That very instant passed –
> On a strange Mob of panting Trees
> And Fences fled away
> And Rivers where the Houses ran
> Those looked that lived – that Day –
> The Bell within the steeple wild
> The flying tidings told –
> How much can come
> And much can go,
> And yet abide the World!
>
> (1593)[58]

The wind announces its sudden overpowering presence by a metallic clamour soon to be answered by the clamour of a church bell gone wild. Necromancy is conveyed by 'a Green Chill upon the Heat' that precedes the lightning bolt ('The Doom's electric Moccasin'); by trees thrashing about and fences demolished; by demonic rivers invading the houses.

Dickinson's apocalyptic imagery in 'There came a Wind like a Bugle – ', Mario L. D'Avanzo has suggested, is illuminated by the early chapters of the Book of Revelation and Ecclesiastes. God advises John of Patmos that he will come, to those not watchful, 'as a thief, and thou shalt not know what hour I will come upon

thee' (Revelation 3:3). The blast of a trumpet precedes each opening
of the seven seals in which God's truth is concealed – and John's
vision of God seated on his throne in heaven refers to 'a rainbow
round about the throne, in sight like unto an emerald' (4:3); and to
'lightnings and thunderings and voices' (4:5). In Dickinson's poem,
it is as if a day of death and judgement has come – and the divine
visitant (likened to 'an Emerald Ghost') cannot be kept out by barred
windows and doors. Dickinson's closing lines seem to echo the
words of the Preacher on the transience of life and the permanence
of the world: 'One generation passeth away, and another generation
cometh: but the earth abideth forever' (Ecclesiastes 1:4).[59] The poem
is by no means a gloss on Revelation and Ecclesiastes; these Biblical
allusions, however, do contribute to what Charles R. Anderson has
called 'the sense of cosmic upheaval' in the poem, the sense of a vast
invisible world that threatens to invade, at any moment, the placid
routine of an ordinary village.[60]

5

When Nathanael first approaches Jesus, he is told things about
himself unknown to anyone else; filled with awe, he calls the Master 'Son of God'. And Jesus replies: 'Because I said unto thee, I
saw thee under the fig tree, believest thou? thou shalt see greater
things than these' (John 1:46–50). Christ's miraculous power to
see the unseeable had its counterpart, in the nineteenth century,
in numerous factual and fictional accounts of psychic powers –
accounts of the uncanny ability of certain individuals to see that
which is not visible to ordinary eyes.

In a climactic episode of *The Blithedale Romance*, Professor
Westervelt tells an audience in a New England village hall 'of
a new era that was dawning upon the world; an era that would
link soul to soul, and the present life to what we call futurity,
with a closeness that should finally convert both worlds into one
great, mutually conscious brotherhood'. It is a new scientific age
and Westervelt describes the advances taking place 'as if it were a
matter of chemical discovery' – referring in his discourse to some
'universally pervasive fluid'. The Veiled Lady is then introduced
and she sits motionless on the platform, oblivious to the shouts of
spectators who have been challenged by Professor Westervelt to
make their presence known to her. She is, the professor explains,

in communion with the spiritual world and even 'The roar of a battery or cannon' could not disturb her trance. 'And yet, were I to will it', he continues, 'sitting in this very hall, she could hear the desert-wind sweeping over the sands, as far off as Arabia . . . .'[61] Through his narrator, Miles Coverdale, Hawthorne conveyed his contempt for Westervelt and other traffickers in the spirit world who were degrading humanity and its religious aspirations ('To hold intercourse with spirits of this order, we must stoop and grovel in some element more vile than earthly dust').[62]

The 'universally pervasive fluid' referred to glowingly by Professor Westervelt (and contemptuously by Miles Coverdale) was the 'mesmeric fluid' of Mesmer or the 'odyle' of Reichenbach – a subtle magnetic force manifesting its presence and power in each human body and throughout the material universe. It was these fluids, the spiritualists claimed, that helped explain thought transference and clairvoyance. Their claims were vigorously denied by most Protestant ministers who, like Charles Beecher in 1853, found spiritualism a 'subtle but genuine materialism' which rejected the authority of the Bible and found all men capable of matching Christ's divine vision.[63] Many adherents of spiritualism were drawn from the ranks of the Universalist ministry; one of them, William Fishbough, announced his disillusionment with the movement in language somewhat similar to that of Miles Coverdale: 'New York [he wrote in 1853] is eminently a superficial, sensual, and practically infidel place, and . . . there are comparatively few spiritualists here who acknowledge the Lord and his providential rule, either in theory or practice.'[64]

There were also many highly regarded Christian leaders in midnineteenth century America who did not traffic in the spirit world or degrade humanity and its religious aspirations – but who spoke in a language of science not unlike that of the sinister Professor Westervelt. One such leader was Edward Hitchcock, a towering presence in Amherst and an important influence on Emily Dickinson.

From early youth, Hitchcock was passionately involved with both religion and science. After serving as a Congregational minister for four years, he resigned to pursue his interest in science – and to accept a post as Professor of Chemistry and Natural History at Amherst College. He was a prime mover in bringing scientific education to the school and, after his inauguration as President in 1845, changed the title of his course because it did not fully convey the grand object he had in view: 'That object', he wrote in *Reminiscences of Amherst College*, 'was to illustrate, by the scientific facts which I taught, the principles of natural theology'. This he felt to be true of all the natural sciences and he now called his course 'a Professorship of Natural Theology and Geology, adding this latter science because I have been in the habit of going more into detail concerning it, and because no science equals this in its religous applications'.[65]

Richard B. Sewall has surveyed Hitchcock's great importance to Amherst – and to Emily Dickinson. During her first term at Mount Holyoke Female Seminary, she heard Hitchcock preach a sermon there on her favorite chapter in the Book of Revelation – chapter 21, the one she later referred to in a letter to Mary Bowles as the 'Gem chapter'. She praised Hitchcock's writings on nature in a letter to Higginson and, along with Austin, seems almost certainly to have read *The Religion of Geology* (1851). 'There are more earthquakes and volcanoes in her poems [Sewall observes] – phenomena which then were central in all geological inquiry, especially Hitchcock's – than in the poetry of Keats, Emerson, Browning, and Shelley combined.' Sewall points to a Dickinson poem that compresses – with what may be an ironical touch – Hitchcock's lengthy argument, in the opening lecture of *The Religion of Geology*, that the findings of modern chemistry have answered the questions of those doubtful about the practical possibility of a resurrection of bodies incinerated in the final conflagration [2 Peter 3:10–11]:

> The Chemical conviction
> That Nought be lost
> Enable in Disaster
> My fractured Trust –
>
> The Faces of the Atoms
> If I shall see
> How more the Finished Creatures
> Departed me!
>
> (954)[66]

'[C]hemistry informs us', asserts Hitchcock in his lecture, 'that no case of combustion, how fiercely soever the fire may rage, annihilates the least particle of matter; and that . . . it is not necessary that the resurrection body should contain a single particle of the matter laid in the grave, in order to be the same body . . . '. Dickinson's persona says that these scientific findings give strength to her insufficient faith – and she seems to convey more of a bemused wonderment about these scientific claims than the 'pointed satire' that David Porter has found in the poem.[67]

Hitchcock's lectures and books aroused considerable controversy. The preface to the 1859 edition of *The Religion of Geology* tells of a lengthy attack on the first edition of the book that gratifies him because the periodical in which it appears, the *Boston Investigator*, is 'rather Atheistic'. Hitchcock then refers to pious critics who think his views are 'quite acceptable to the Infidel and Atheist' – and quotes a letter from an Englishman (apparently a clergyman) who informs him: 'I cannot but behold you in the fearfully perilous circumstances of having made yourself an antagonist to God.' Which camp can we believe, he asks: 'The Infidel raves furiously, because I have endeavored to make Geology sustain and illustrate revelation; but my Christian friend declares my book to be thoroughy infidel.' He concludes his preface (dated from Amherst College on 1 June 1859) with the observation that 'the two attacks neutralize each other, and leave me unharmed'.[68]

An especially startling lecture in *The Religion of Geology*, delivered in about 1850, is titled 'The Telegraphic System of the Universe';[69] in it, Hitchcock makes clear his close connections to spiritualism and mesmerism – a connection that helps explain the controversy that his book aroused. The lecture also sheds light on important aspects of Dickinson's mind and art.

'The Telegraphic System of the Universe' opens with a reference to a common tendency among men: Our tendency to refer to inanimate objects surrounding us as capable of seeing and hearing – of bearing witness to the truth. The most striking illustrations of these powerful figurative representations are to be found in sacred Scripture. To make certain that his people keeps their sacred covenant with God, Joshua sets a great stone under an oak and tells the Israelites: '*Behold, this stone shall be a witness unto us. For it hath heard all the words of the Lord which he spake unto us. It shall, therefore, be a witness unto you, lest ye deny your God*' [Joshua 24:27]. When some of the Pharisees ask Jesus to rebuke his disciples if they do not pay him homage as he passes among them, he replies: '*If these should hold their peace, the stones would immediately cry out*' [Luke 19:40].[70]

These ancient, apparently figurative illustrations, Hitchcock proposes, have been given literal confirmation by recent discoveries of modern science. We now know that all our words and actions leave a record in the material universe, a record so absorbed into its very texture that it can never be obliterated; we also know 'that nature, through all time, is ever ready to bear testimony of what we have said and done'. Hitchcock sums up his view with a forceful flourish (the emphasis and typographical display are his):

> The principle which I advance in its naked form is this: *Our words, our actions, and even our thoughts make an indelible impression on the universe.* This principle converts creation

> > INTO A VAST SOUNDING GALLERY;
> > INTO A VAST PICTURE GALLERY;
> > AND INTO A UNIVERSAL TELEGRAPH.

> This proposition I shall endeavor to sustain by an appeal to well-established principles of science.[71]

Among the scientific principles that lend support to this view of the telegraphic system of the universe, says Hitchcock, is 'the odylic reaction', a new branch of science developed by Baron Reichenbach and described in his *Researches on Magnetism . . . in their Relations to the Vital Force*, recently translated into English. Reichenbach's experiments seem to demonstrate the presence in all bodies throughout the universe of a distinctive force, or *odyle*, analogous to electricity and magnetism. Some of the most distinguished scientists in Europe have expressed confidence in Reichenbach – and in findings 'that promise to explain philosophically . . . the phenomena of mesmerism, without a resort to superhuman agency, either satanic or angelic'. Through his experiments, Reichenbach has tried to demonstrate 'that even the light of the stars exerted an odylic influence upon the human system; that is, certain effects independent altogether of their light . . . '. If there is no mistake in these experiments, Hitchcock concludes, the fact of this odylic influence almost certainly means 'that beings in other spheres may possess such an exaltation of sensibilities as to be able to learn what is going on in this world, and that it is easy to conceive how our sensorium may be raised to the same exalted pitch'.[72]

The term *sensorium*, as defined in Dickinson's lexicon, is 'the seat of sense and perception'; the *OED* quotes the seventeenth-century Cambridge Platonist and mystic Henry More: 'For there is first a tactual conjunction as it were of the representative rayes of everything, with our sensorium before we know the things themselves.' Dickinson was highly responsive to Hitchcock's religious and scientific views – and in numerous poems she seems to be dramatising the extremely exalted pitch to which the sensorium may be raised.

6

A poem written about 1861 seems to invoke the 'beings in other spheres' mentioned by Edward Hitchcock in 'The Telegraphic System of the Universe':

> Alone, I cannot be –
> The Hosts – do visit me –
> Recordless Company –
> Who baffle Key –
>
> They have no Robes, nor Names –
> No Almanacs – nor Climes –
> But general Homes
> Like Gnomes –
>
> Their Coming, may be known
> By Couriers within –
> Their going – is not –
> For they're never gone –
>
> (298)[73]

These ghostly visitors are a recordless company, without robes or names – unlike the spirits of loved ones sought out by Higginson, Barrett Browning, Ruskin; and the sacred mysteries experienced by Dickinson's persona are more baffling and profound than those reported by the mediums they consulted. They have made their visitation known to the speaker 'By Couriers within – ' (perhaps Dickinson's trope for what Hitchcock called 'our sensorium . . . raised to the same exalted pitch'). These mysterious presences are not invaders, but cordially received visitors who, Theodora Ward suggests, spurred the poet 'to work at her craft with full acceptance of her creative gift'.[74]

Hitchcock opens *The Religon of Geology* with a dedicatory note to his wife informing her that 'There are ties which death cannot break; and we indulge the hope that by them we shall be linked together and to the throne of God through eternal ages'.[75] In all his teaching and writings, Hitchcock dwelled repeatedly on the Resurrection – and on its emblematic manifestations in nature.[76]

Dickinson knew his writings well and reported to Higginson on one occasion: 'When Flowers annually died and I was a child, I used to read Dr Hitchcock's Book on the Flowers of North America. This comforted their Absence – assuring me they lived' (L488). Dickinson's 'They put Us far apart – ' is a resurrection hymn (in Watts's Short Metre) depicting the triumphant martyrdom of lovers separated by a terrible war – in Hitchcock's 'Telegraphic System of the Universe':

> They put Us far apart –
> As separate as Sea
> And Her unsown Peninsula –
> We signified "These see" –
>
> They took away our Eyes –
> They thwarted Us with Guns –
> "I see Thee" each responded straight
> Through Telegraphic Signs –
>
> With Dungeons – They devised –
> But through their thickest skill –
> And their opaquest Adamant –
> Our Souls saw – just as well –
>
> They summoned Us to die –
> With sweet alacrity
> We stood upon our stapled feet –
> Condemned – but just – to see –
>
> Permission to recant –
> Permission to forget –
> We turned our backs upon the Sun
> For perjury of that –
>
> Not Either – noticed Death –
> Of Paradise – aware –
> Each other's Face – was all the Disc
> Each other's setting – saw –
>
> (474)[77]

The transcendent triumph of lovers over the powerful earthly forces that vainly seek to keep them apart is set forth in a series of paradoxical conceits reminiscent of the metaphysical poets she admired. Louis L. Martz's comment on Donne's 'The Extasie' ('the poem maintains a complex tone in which the playful and the solemn, the profane and the sacred, are held in a perilous poise')[78] seems equally applicable to 'They put Us far apart – '. But the distinctive imagery and power of Dickinson's poem draw on influences closer to her own life and time. A great war was in progress – a war that had exiled her beloved minister to a remote place. The metaphoric flights that depict the suffering and transcendent victory of the lovers over those who separate them are interspersed with references to 'Guns' and 'Telegraphic Signs' that were all too real to Dickinson and the nation in 1862.[79] (The metaphysical implications of 'Telegraphic Signs' had been thoroughly explored, a decade before Dickinson wrote her poem, by Edward Hitchcock.)[80]

Seated in a New England village hall, the entranced Veiled Lady of *The Blithedale Romance* is able to hear the desert wind sweeping over the sands of Arabia. In 'I see thee better – in the Dark – ' it is not malevolent mesmerism but the power of love that so intensifies the vision of Dickinson's persona that she is able to see beyond the grave:

> I see thee better – in the Dark –
> I do not need a Light –
> The Love of Thee – a Prism be –
> Excelling Violet –
>
> I see thee better for the Years
> That hunch themselves between –
> The Miner's Lamp – sufficient be –
> To nullify the Mine –
>
> And in the Grave – I see Thee best –
> It's little Panels be
> Aglow – All ruddy – with the Light
> I held so high, for Thee –
>
> What need of Day –
> To Those whose Dark – hath so – surpassing
>   Sun –
> It deem it be – Continually –
> At the Meridian?
>
> (611)[81]

In 'The Telegraphic System of the Universe', Hitchcock tells of 'a power in nature capable of impressing the outlines of some objects upon others in total darkness' – and of a power in each of us (a 'sensorium' raised to an exalted pitch) that enables us to see beyond the grave.[82] In Dickinson's poem, love as a prism is a powerful trope – and the natural world is encompassed by the spirit world.

7

The Veiled Lady, in Hawthorne's romance, is an immediate ancestor of Egeria Boynton, in Howells' *The Undiscovered Country*, who can see objects hidden from her view – but only when her eyes are bandaged.[83] In 'What Did She See With?' – a story by Elizabeth Stuart Phelps that appeared in the *Atlantic* in 1866—a young servant girl suddenly acquires psychic powers after a near-fatal illness: On one occasion, she 'sees' (with closed eyes) a missing earring buried under deep snow; on another, she 'witnesses' a burglary in progress in a remote part of the house. The story closes with an even more astounding clairvoyant vision: She 'sees' a relative of the family – missing and believed dead after the watery plunge of a railroad car – alive in a Western town seven hundred miles away.[84]

During the war, Emily Dickinson had lived with her Norcross cousins while she was undergoing eye treatments in Boston. Two decades later, she wrote to tell them that she was reading a popular novel of the day, Hugh Conway's *Called Back*, and finding it 'haunting' and 'impressive' (L962).[85] Shortly before she lapsed into the coma that ended her life, she scrawled her last letter – a message to her cousins consisting of just two words: 'Called back.' (L1046) A brief account of Conway's melodramatic novel readily reveals why she found it engrossing – and why she drew on its title for the message she sent her cousins while confronting the ultimate crisis of her life.

The narrator of *Called Back*, Gilbert Vaughan, gives harrowing details about eye treatments for an affliction that leaves him, for a time, totally blind. He 'witnesses', as a sightless bystander, a terrible crime. His sight restored, he is guided back to the scene of the crime by the woman he loves, Pauline March. She had also been a witness to the same crime, the murder of her brother, and is suffering from an amnesia induced by the shock of what she saw. Now his beloved serves as a medium for a spectral reenactment of the crime: The narrator is 'called back' to that which he had previously 'seen'; the young woman he loves is 'called back' from her mental darkness by the power of love and music. (She had been playing the piano and singing at the time of the crime: it is the touch of the narrator's hand and the sounding of a chord on the same piano that empowers her to call back the terrible scene.) After numerous complications, Gilbert Vaughan penetrates the mystery surrounding the crime and tracks down the criminals. And the empty marriage of Gilbert and Pauline, contracted while she was mentally afflicted, is transformed into a true union.

A pivotal episode in *Called Back* is the eerie reenactment of the crime; it is of crucial importance to Pauline's return from mental darkness. How can it be explained? Gilbert Vaughan can find no explanation. But he is certain that what he is experiencing is no hallucination or dream – for the same scene is acted out each time he takes Pauline's hand into his own:

> Not once, not twice, but many times did this occur, until skeptical as I was, as even I am now in such matters, I could only believe that in some mysterious way I was actually gazing on the very sight which had met the girl's eyes when memory, perhaps mercifully, fled from her, and reason was left impaired . . . . Call it cataleptic, clairvoyant, any thing you will, but it was as I relate.[86]

It is understandable that Conway's novel – centered as it was on blindness and violence, on spectral visions and the redemptive power of love – would be 'haunting' and 'impressive' to Emily Dickinson, that its two-word title would serve as her last message.[87]

*   *   *

In his essay 'Illusions', Emerson pictured man engulfed by 'pillows of illusions' (as thick 'as flakes in a snow-storm'), groping from childhood to old age through an elaborate lifelong masquerade in which all, or almost all, participate as masquers and dupes ('The intellectual man requires a fine bait; the sots are easily amused'). But in the midst of this 'snow-storm of illusions', Emerson concludes, there were the gods still sitting around, on their thrones – there waiting for him who 'fixes his fortune in absolute Nature'.[88] Emily Dickinson would never find it possible to fix her fortune in absolute Nature – or in any other Absolute. She was drawn to the passionate religious convictions of Charles Wadsworth, Thomas Wentworth Higginson and Edward Hitchcock; but she fixed her fortune in her own wide-ranging explorations – in her own existential grapplings with everyday experience ('Drama's Vitallest Expression is the Common Day'), with the mysteries of the fields and skies outside her house, with the shaping of words and sounds into hymnlike poems. Resurrection hymns alternated with cries of doubt and anguish. 'Rest would come only with certitude', observes Albert Gelpi, 'and on her lonely exploration she would never find the miraculous Fleece that would end the quest'.[89]

Her quest was not as lonely or idiosyncratic as we have been led to believe. She shared with family and friends (Wadsworth and Higginson foremost among them) her life and thought and poems – and her lifelong search for answers to unanswerable questions. She experienced with them (and through them) a terrible war. She shared with these kindred spirits her passion for sacred books – and her passionate dedication to a sacred vocation. The uncompromising honesty of her quest has spoken eloquently to our time.

Notes

PROLOGUE: 'IMMURED IN HEAVEN!'

1. Quotations from Dickinson's poems and letters are from the editions of Thomas H. Johnson, *The Poems of Emily Dickinson*, 3 vols (Cambridge, Mass.: The Belknap Press of Harvard Univ. Press, 1955) and *The Letters of Emily Dickinson*, 3 vols. (Cambridge, Mass.: The Belknap Press of Harvard Univ. Press, 1958; parenthetical numbers (letter numbers are preceded by 'L') in the text refer to poem and letter numbers assigned by Johnson. 'PF' followed by a number refers to Prose Fragments and the numbers assigned to them by Johnson (in the third volume of the *Letters*).
2. Jay Leyda, *The Years and Hours of Emily Dickinson* (New Haven, Conn.: Yale Univ. Press, 1960), II, 406; the following entry is on the same page.
3. Ibid.
4. Barton Levi St Armand has suggested that Dickinson's letter and enclosed elegy reflect the poet's involvement with the popular gospel of consolation as disseminated by Lydia Sigourney and others: 'To Dickinson as to Sigourney, the loved dead were astral guides and spiritual mediums to a better world. ' *Emily Dickinson and Her Culture: The Soul's Society* (Cambridge: Cambridge Univ. Press, 1984), p. 47; but St Armand also emphasises (p. 24) the poet's creative use of pervasive sentimental views.
5. Richard B. Sewall, *The Life of Emily Dickinson* (New York: Farrar, Straus and Giroux, 1974), I, 204–5; Sewall is referring to the first elegiac letter and poem ('Pass to thy Rendezvous of Light') sent after Gilbert's death – but his observation also applies to the elegies that followed, including 'Immured in Heaven!' In a similar vein, Charles R. Anderson has described 'Pass to thy Rendezvous of Light' as 'more a poem than a personal lament . . . '. See Anderson, *Emily Dickinson's Poetry: Stairway of Surprise* (New York: Holt, Rinehart and Winston, 1960), p. 226. For the view that Dickinson's letter to Sue and poem ('Pass to thy Rendezvous of Light') make 'abundantly clear' Dickinson's belief in immortality, see Peggy Anderson, 'The Bride of the White Election: A New Look at Biblical Influence on Emily Dickinson', in *Nineteenth Century Women Writers of the English-Speaking World*, ed. Rhoda B. Nathan (New York: Greenwood Press, 1986), p. 3.
6. Leyda, *Years and Hours*, II, 410.
7. Thomas H. Johnson, *Emily Dickinson: An Interpretive Biography* (Cambridge, Mass.: The Belknap Press of Harvard Univ. Press, 1955), pp. 229–30.

CHAPTER ONE: A MINISTER IN EXILE:
A MINISTER REMEMBERED

1. A beginning point among the numerous discussions of these letters is Sewall's chapter, 'The Master Letters', in his *Life*, II, 512–31; and R. W. Franklin's Introduction to his edition of *The Master Letters of Emily Dickinson* (Amherst, Mass.: Amherst College Press, 1986), pp. 5–10. My quotations from the Master letters are from this edition and are identifed in the text by parenthetical page numbers preceded by 'ML'. Among those who have speculated about Dickinson's 'terror', Millicent Todd Bingham and Thomas H. Johnson have linked her distress to Wadsworth's acceptance of a call to Calvary Church in San Francisco; Bingham, *Emily Dickinson's Home* (New York: Harper & Brothers, 1955), pp. 419–20 and Johnson, *Emily Dickinson*, p. 81. Richard B. Sewall has suggested that Dickinson's eye troubles and 'the threatened loss of her power to read' is a more plausible explanation; Sewall, *The Lyman Letters: New Light on Emily Dickinson and Her Family* (Amherst: Univ. of Massachusetts Press, 1965), p. 74.

2. For the view that Wadsworth was Dickinson's 'Master', see William R. Sherwood, *Circumference and Circumstance: Stages in the Mind and Art of Emily Dickinson* (New York: Columbia Univ. Press, 1968), pp. 69–77; and Vivian R. Pollak, *Dickinson: The Anxiety of Gender* (Ithaca, N.Y.: Cornell Univ. Press, 1984), esp. pp. 96–100. Among others, David Higgins, *Portrait of Emily Dickinson: The Poet and Her Prose* (Rutgers, N.J.: Rutgers Univ. Press, 1967), esp. pp. 116–19, has presented the case for Bowles. For Judge Lord as 'Master', see John Evangelist Walsh, *The Hidden Life of Emily Dickinson* (New York: Simon and Schuster, 1971), esp. pp. 187–9. For the view that the letters may have been addressed to herself, see Albert Gelpi, *The Tenth Muse: The Psyche of the American Poet* (Cambridge, Mass. : Harvard Univ. Press, 1975), pp. 255–6; for Martha Nell Smith's discussion, see her '"Rowing in Eden": Gender and the Poetics of Emily Dickinson' (Ph. D. diss., Rutgers University, 1985), pp. 15–36.

3. Two such accounts are those of Martha Dickinson Bianchi, *The Life and Letters of Emily Dickinson* (Boston: Houghton, Mifflin and Company, 1924), pp. 46–7; and William H. Shurr, *The Marriage of Emily Dickinson: A Study of the Fascicles* (n.p.: The Univ. of Kentucky Press, 1983), esp. pp. 170–8. In Bianchi's version, there is a fateful meeting after Emily Dickinson heard the minister preach in Philadelphia, and a love that was mutual and overwhelming; but when she would not say 'the one word he implored', he resigned his ministry to resettle in a distant city, a continent away. In Shurr's version, the lovers consummate their mystical marriage in a physical union and, after Emily Dickinson experiences a pregnancy and abortion, finally agree

to a lifelong separation on earth – and, ultimately, a fulfillment of their union in heaven. For a cogent comment on some of Shurr's misreadings of poems, see David Porter, 'Dickinson's Readers', *New England Quarterly*, 57 (1984), 114. Shurr (*Marriage*, p. 124) says about Wadsworth's move to California: 'In 1862 Wadsworth abruptly decamped, moving himself and his family from a successful practice in Philadelphia all the way to the frontier city of San Francisco, where he was installed as pastor of the Calvary Church in November of 1862'. For a very different account of Wadsworth's move, see section 5 of this chapter.

4. George F. Whicher, *This Was a Poet: Emily Dickinson* (Ann Arbor: Univ. of Michigan Press, 1957), p. 101.
5. Leyda, *Years and Hours*, II, 112.
6. Whicher, *This Was a Poet*, p. 102; Wadsworth's reclusive traits are dwelled on in funeral tributes to the dead minister (see below, section 9).
7. Leyda, *Years and Hours*, I, 353.
8. Richard B. Sewall has linked the passage from Wadsworth's 'The Gospel Call' to Emily Dickinson's 'Me – come! My Dazzled face'; but I find unconvincing his suggestion that Dickinson is primarily concerned in the poem with the immortality of being remembered for her poetry. Sewall, *Life*, I, 456–7; Sewall discusses possible echoes of Wadsworth in several other Dickinson poems on pp. 455–6, 457–9. For an earlier discussion of Wadsworth's influence, see Mary Elizabeth Barbot, 'Emily Dickinson Parallels', *New England Quarterly*, 14 (1941), 689–92. The quoted passage from 'The Mortal Immortalized' is in Wadsworth, *Sermons* (New York and San Francisco: A. Roman & Company, 1869), p. 235.
9. See Sewall, *Life*, pp. 688–94; the importance of Thomas à Kempis to Dickinson is discussed further in my Chapter Two, section 7.
10. John W. Nevin, *The Mystical Presence and Other Writings on the Eucharist*, ed. Bard Thompson and George H. Bricker (Philadelphia: United Church Press, 1966), p. 23; for the controversy over the Lord's Supper, see Julius Melton, *Presbyterian Worship in America: Changing Patterns Since 1787* (Richmond, Va: John Knox Press, 1967), esp. pp. 39–41.
11. Wadsworth, *Sermons* (1869), p. 129.
12. Ibid. , pp. 221–22, 230.
13. [George Burrowes], *Impressions of Dr. Wadsworth as a Preacher* (San Francisco: Towne & Bacon, 1863), pp. 10–11, 12–13, 15–17.
14. Leyda, *Years and Hours*, I, 352.
15. Ibid., p. 353.
16 Dr William Scott Wadsworth (1868–1955) informed his friend Dr G. Hall Todd, pastor of the Arch Street Presbyterian Church, about his father's friendship with Dr Scott – and about being named after Dr Scott. Letters to me from Dr Todd, 24 November and 8 December 1980. For details about Dr Scott's service as pastor of Calvary Presbyterian Church, see Clifford M. Drury, *William Anderson Scott: "No Ordinary Man"* (Glendale, Cal.: Arthur H. Clark,

1967), pp. 149–267; an account of Scott's resignation and of the published reports concerning it are on pp. 252–3. The date of the congregational election of Dr Wadsworth as the new pastor of Calvary Church is reported in the *Encyclopaedia of the Presbyterian Church*, ed. Alfred Nevin (Philadelphia: Presbyterian Encyclopaedia Publishing Company, 1884), p. 804. My belief that the friendship between Scott and Wadsworth had its beginnings in Philadelphia in the late 1850s is based on the fact that there seems to have been no possibility of a later meeting – prior to the birth and christening of Wadsworth's son in early 1868. Wadsworth came to San Francisco several months after Scott's precipitous departure on 1 October 1861; Scott returned to San Francisco shortly after Wadsworth left Calvary Church in May of 1869 to return to Philadelphia. Wadsworth's tribute to Scott in the naming of his son (in early 1868) might have been based on an epistolary friendship – but the evidence points to a meeting in Philadelphia during one of Scott's visits before the war. For details about the movements of the two ministers, see Drury, *William Anderson Scott*, esp. pp. 269–70, 292, 294; for Wadsworth's arrival in San Francisco, see Leyda, *Years and Hours*, II, 57 and the *Encyclopaedia of the Presbyterian Church*, p. 804. Details about Wadsworth's career after his return to Philadelphia are to be found in Vivian R. Pollak, 'After Calvary: The Last Years of ED's "Dearest Earthly Friend"', *Dickinson Studies*, No. 34 (1978), 13–18.

17. Drury, *William Anderson Scott*, pp. 240–1, 256, 258–67, 269; for Scott's own account of these turbulent events, see [William Anderson Scott], *My Residence in and Departure from California* (Paris: E. Brière, 1861), pp. 2–3.

18. Wadsworth, *Our Own Sins* (Philadelphia: King & Baird, 1861), pp. 5, 7, 10–13, 15ff.

19. Letter to me from Dr G. Hall Todd, 14 November 1980.

20. Like the nation, Philadelphia – and the Presbyterian Church – was deeply divided on the issue of slavery. On the same Fast Day (4 January) in which Wadsworth inveighed against 'self-righteous hypocrisy', another Presbyterian minister in another part of the city called slavery a sin for which God was punishing our nation. See George Duffield, Jr, *The God of Our Fathers* (Philadelphia: T. B. Pugh, 1861); the sermon was preached in the Coates Street Presbyterian Church. For details about this sermon, see George M. Marsden, *The Evangelical Mind and the New School Presbyterian Experience* (New Haven, Conn. : Yale Univ. Press, 1970), pp. 202–3. Mobs visited the offices of suspected Southern-sympathising publications, including the Presbyterian *Christian Observer*, to enforce a public display of the national flag. See William Dusinberre, *Civil War Issues in Philadelphia, 1856–1865* (Philadelphia: Univ. of Pennsylvania Press, 1965), pp. 117–18.

21. Wadsworth, *The Christian Soldier* (Philadelphia: Lindsay & Blakeston, 1861), p. 21; Wadsworth, *Thanksgiving* (Philadelphia: Peterson & Brothers, 1861), pp. 22–3. (The sermon was delivered on 28 November 1861.)

22. Karen Dandurand, 'Why Dickinson Did Not Publish' (Ph.D. diss., University of Massachusetts, 1984), pp. 126–7.
23. Quoted in Sewall, *Life*, II, 689; for a further discussion of the importance of the *Imitation* to Dickinson, see my Chapter 2, section 7.
24. Sandra Gilbert and Susan Gubar, *The Madwoman in the Attic: The Woman Writer and the Nineteenth Century Literary Imagination* (New Haven, Conn.: Yale Univ. Press, 1979), p. 607.
25. Dickinson conveys this exchange of bodies by a trope referring to the facial hair (and coarse skin) of men:

> I dont know what you can do for it – thank you – Master – but if I had the Beard – on my cheek – like you – and you – had Daisy's petals – and you cared so for me – what would become of you? (ML 39–40)

This passage poses a problem to Vivian R. Pollak (among other critics) in her consideration of the likelihood that Wadsworth is Dickinson's 'Master': 'We know that ["Master"] had a beard' – and extant photographs of Wadsworth 'show him without a beard' (Pollak, *Anxiety of Gender*, pp. 95, 99). I would suggest that Dickinson's trope for an exchange of bodies and genders does not rule out Wadsworth. Every man (however recent his shave) has a beard – and every never-shaven woman has not; a stroke of the hand confirms this. That Dickinson used the word *beard* or *bearded* as a trope for the male gender is confirmed by a letter to her nephew Ned (written shortly before her death), apparently in response to a gift or communication from him:

> What an Embassy –
> What an Ambassador!
> "And pays his Heart for what his Eyes eat only!"
> Excuse the bearded Pronoun –
> > Ever,
> > Aunt Emily
> >
> > (L1026)

She is apologising for applying to herself a pronoun referring to Antony – in Enobarbus' speech (*Antony and Cleopatra*, II.ii.222–6): 'Our courteous Antony, . . . / Being barber'd ten times o'er, goes to the feast; / And for his ordinary pays his heart / For what his eyes eat only.'
    Martha Nell Smith calls attention to the fact that when Dickinson 'first penned "but if I had the Beard on my cheek," she did not add "like you – "'; these words, inserted in pencil, suggests Smith, are 'written in a peculiar hand (either added by Dickinson at a quite later time or inserted by someone else) and pencilled above the line,

apparently an afterthought'. Smith offers this revision as evidence
for the possibility that the letter might be addressed to a woman
– and Dickinson is asking: 'What if I were a man and our love a
usual heterosexual arrangement?' (Smith, '"Rowing in Eden"', pp.
24–5). The added pencilled words 'like you', however, are quite
consistent with Dickinson's handwriting in this same letter: The
word *you* is identically written two lines below; and the same is
true of the word *like* as it appears on the following page; see the
facsimile of this letter reproduced (as are the others) in Franklin's
edition (ML, 41, 42). Since the words immediately following those
that talk about a beard fantasise a Master without a beard ('and
you – had Daisy's petals – '), there would seem confirmation that
this letter is addressed to a man. Smith agrees to the likelihood
of this but also explores the possibility that Dickinson, as she
does elsewhere, is approaching 'a beloved woman with masculine
address' (pp. 24, 25–6).

26.   Drury, *William Anderson Scott*, pp. 246, 249.
27.   George S. Merriam, *The Life and Times of Samuel Bowles* (New York:
       The Century Co. , 1885), II, 2.
28.   For the quotation from More, see the entry for 'corporation' in
       the *Oxford English Dictionary*; the reference to the king as Cor-
       poration is from an Elizabethan commentator quoted in Ernst H.
       Kantorowicz, *The King's Two Bodies: A Study in Mediaeval Political
       Theology* (Princeton, N.J.: Princeton Univ. Press, 1957), p. 24; for the
       tendency of American churches to form corporations, see ibid., pp.
       404–5. (I wish to thank Joseph Lease for calling my attention to this
       important book.)
       Kantorowicz opens his massive study of these topics with an
       anecdote bearing directly on Emily Dickinson's use of the term:

> One day I found in my mail an offprint from a liturgical periodical
> published by a Benedictine Abbey in the United States, which bore
> the publisher's imprint: *The Order of St. Benedict, Inc.* To a scholar
> coming from the European Continent . . . , nothing could have
> been more baffling than to find the abbreviation *Inc.*, customary
> with business and other corporations, attached to the venerable
> community founded by St. Benedict on the rock of Montecassino
> in the very year in which Justinian abolished the Platonic Acad-
> emy in Athens. (Ibid., p. vii)

       Kantorowicz's book is an extended and illuminating response to this
       puzzling phenomenon. James Madison had vigorously opposed the
       incorporation by the Federal government of religious institutions
       believing it an enemy of the 'wall of separation' between Church
       and State; but by the mid-nineteenth century, as Kantorowicz puts
       it, 'secular [state] corporational law had its retroactive effects on the
       status of the church: in fact, the canonistic doctrine has run the
       full circle'. Anson Phelps Stokes and Leo Pfeffer, *Church and State*

in the United States (New York: Harper & Row, 1964), p. 61; and Kantorowicz, *King's Two Bodies*, p. 405.

For a typical legislative enactment during this period, see 'RELIGIOUS CORPORATIONS / AN ACT concerning corporations. Laws 1871–72', in Illinois Revised Statutes (St. Paul, Minn.: West Publishing Company, 1979), IV, 1476.

Richard B. Sewall, one of the few commentators to take note of this important term, overlooks its religious meaning and sees it as evidence against Wadsworth and for Bowles as Emily Dickinson's 'Master': 'She speaks of the "Corporation" going to Heaven, a more likely term to use to a man of affairs like Bowles, whose SAMUEL BOWLES AND COMPANY topped the masthead on every issue of the *Republican*, than to a minister.' Sewall, *Life*, II, 524.

29. See the entry for 'sequester' in the *Oxford English Dictionary*; among the sources cited is Thomas à Kempis.

30. In a cancelled passage, Dickinson intimates this – but puts the matter somewhat more equivocally: 'Would it do harm – yet we both fear God – '

31. Johnson dates the poem 'late in 1861', Franklin in 'About 1861'; *Poems*, I, 250 and *Manuscript Books*, I, 258. These assigned dates refer to the time a poem is copied; it might, of course, have been copied from a version written earlier in work sheets no longer in existence. R. W. Franklin has offered evidence that Dickinson's copying of poems 'was systematic and may have kept up fairly well with her poetic production'. See Franklin's Introduction to *Manuscript Books*, I, xv–xvi. Cynthia Griffin Wolff has argued that Dickinson accelerated the pace of gathering and copying poems possibly written much earlier; see Wolff, *Emily Dickinson* (New York: Alfred A. Knopf, 1986), p. 576. Franklin's new dating of this Master letter (in *'summer 1861'*) adds to the likelihood that it can be linked to 'There came a Day – at Summer's full' – and lends support to the likelihood that poems written in this period were copied soon after they were written.

32. Merriam, *Life and Times*, I, 330–1; for references to the babies lost at birth, see Leyda, *Years and Hours*, I, xxxiii; Emily Dickinson's letter of consolation (L216); and Merriam, *Life and Times*, I, 311.

33. Merriam, *Life and Times*, I, 330–1.

34. *Letters*, II, 391.

35. Emily Dickinson is responding in this letter to Sue – written about 1884 – to her sister-in-law's request for materials about Bowles ('Go to my Mine as to your own, only more unsparingly – '); Sue had received a letter from George S. Merriam, then preparing a biography of Bowles.

36. Emily Dickinson apparently mistook the date of Bowles's return from California, which took place before the publication of *Daniel Deronda*, for a later trip; see Johnson, *Letters*, III, 865.

37. Merriam, *Life and Times*, II, 63.

38. For details, see Leyda, *Years and Hours*, I, lxxviii–lxxix and (for the crisis in the marriage) II, 129–30. See also the index to Merriam's

biography for Maria Whitney's close association with Bowles and
the Bowles family; Merriam reproduces numerous lengthy extracts
from Bowles's extensive correspondence with Maria Whitney, from
January 1861 to the time of his final illness in 1877 – some of them
surprisingly intimate. Maria Whitney insisted on deleting passages
in Emily Dickinson's letters to her that 'referred to a warmth of
admiration for her on the part of Samuel Bowles' before consenting
to their publication; see Millicent Todd Bingham, *Ancestors' Brocades:
The Literary Debut of Emily Dickinson* (New York: Harper & Brothers,
1945), p. 257. Maria Whitney visited Bowles as he lay dying; see
Merriam, *Life and Letters*, II, 435.

39.   In Montgomery's hymn, the martyrs finally emerge victorious:

> These through fiery trials trod
> These from great affliction came;
> Now before the throne of God,
> Sealed with his almighty name;
> Clad in raiment pure and white . . . .

The edition of Watts's hymns known to Emily Dickinson included
this and other Montgomery hymns; she wrote to her cousins, after
her father's death, that 'Almost the last tune that he heard was
[Montgomery's], "Rest from thy loved employ"' (L414). The poet's
familiarity with Montgomery's hymns had been earlier evidenced
when she quoted from his 'O where shall rest be found' in a letter
to Sue sent in late 1854; see *Letters*, I, 311–12. See *Psalms, Hymns and
Spiritual Songs of the Rev. Isaac Watts, D. D.*, ed. Samuel M. Worcester
(Boston: Crocker & Brewster, 1862), pp. 717, 679.

40.   The article appeared in the *Republican* on 29 March, 1862; Dandurand,
        'Why Dickinson Did Not Publish', pp. 127–8, 126.
41.   Watts, 'When God revealed his gracious name', *Psalms*, p. 253.
42.   Leyda, *Years and Hours*, II, 359–60.
43.   *Funeral Services of the Rev. Charles Wadsworth, D. D.* (Philadelphia: The
        Presbyterian Printing Co., 1882), pp. 22–4.
44.   Ibid., pp. [15]–16; the following quotations are on pp. 26–7.
45.   Ibid., p. 23.
46.   Ibid., p. 30.
47.   Ibid.
48.   Leyda, *Years and Hours*, II, 376; Sewall, *Life*, I, 278, 217–18.
49.   At about the same time this poem was sent to Charles Clark, she
        transmitted to Sue a message that might solace the grieving mother
        – and another elegy on the dead boy that incorporates the concluding
        lines of 'The Spirit lasts – but in what mode – ' The poem is preceded
        by the consoling promise that 'Hopelessness in it's first Film has not
        leave to last – That would close the Spirit, and no intercession could
        do that – '; it opens:

> Expanse cannot be lost –

Not Joy but a Decree
Is Deity –
His Scene, Infinity –

(L871)

This opening stanza closes with the lines about 'Rumor's Gate'
that conclude the poem sent to Clark. Gilbert's death is linked, by
Dickinson, to that of Wadsworth.

50. [George Burrowes], *Impressions of Dr. Wadsworth*, pp. 5, 14, 15; *Funeral Services*, pp. 26, 16.

51. According to Jane Donahue Eberwein, 'Obtaining but our own Extent' commemorates Charles Wadsworth – and is the one poem concerned with both the wonder of the Resurrection of Christ and the possibility of human growth and expansion 'into the mysterious space outside'; Eberwein, *Dickinson: Strategies of Limitation* (Amherst: Univ. of Massachusetts Press, 1985), p. 252.

CHAPTER TWO: SACRED TEXTS TRANSFORMED

1. Similar extravagant tributes to Shakespeare were conveyed to Joseph Lyman ('Why need we Joseph read anything else but him') and F. B. Sanborn (' . . . he has had his Future who has found Shakespeare – ' [L402]). Sewall, *Lyman Letters*, p. 76.

2. Variations on the phrase, 'honour's pawn', occur in several other plays – but never more than once in each play. See Sewall, *Life*, II, 541n. For another echo of *Richard II*, see Jack L. Capps, *Emily Dickinson's Reading, 1836–1886* (Cambridge, Mass.: Harvard Univ. Press, 1966), p. 65.

3. Kantorowicz, *King's Two Bodies*, p. 26.

4. Tillyard, *Shakespeare's History Plays* (New York: Collier Books, 1962), p. 289.

5. Kantorowicz, *King's Two Bodies*, pp. 209, 208, 210.

6. Johnson and Franklin date the poem in about 1861; *Poems*, I, 195 and *Manuscript Books*, I, 226.

7. Bingham, *Ancestor's Brocades*, pp. 141, 144.

8. Vivian R. Pollak observes that 'in subordinating herself to her Master, she liberates herself from other forms of subordination. Acquiescing in his power, she participates decisively in it . . . .' Pollak, *Anxiety of Gender*, p. 168. Pollak refers to the Master here as 'brutal'; St Armand calls him 'peremptory and elusive' (*Soul's Society*, p. 146). In *Macbeth*, a play Dickinson knew well and frequently cited, Caithness takes note of the misrule of the bloody usurper: 'He cannot buckle his distemper'd cause / Within the belt of rule' (V.ii.17–18) Implied in Dickinson's poem is both fealty and sacred partnership that set the speaker and her royal Master apart from the world.

9. Johnson and Franklin date the poem in about 1862; *Poems*, II, 389 and *Manuscript Books*, I, 354.

10.   Franklin dates the Master letter ('Oh – did I offend it') in early 1861 because it was written 'at a point of transition' in her handwriting: the instances of the word *the* show the forms nearly balanced in number (6 unlinked, 8 linked). (ML, 8) Both Johnson and Franklin date the poem in about 1861; *Poems*, I, 196 and *Manuscript Books*, I, 226. The handwriting in the manuscript poem 'Doubt Me! My Dim Companion!' reveals a transitional state similar to that of the Master letter: There are six instances of the word *the* – three linked and three unlinked. See *Manuscript Books*, I, 249–50. For the likelihood that the poems of this period were written and copied at about the same time, see above, Chapter One, n. 31. William H. Shurr reads the poem as a response to Wadsworth's 'doubt' about the reality of her love because she is holding back from physical intimacy with him (*Marriage*, pp. 72–3); but the first two stanzas refer to the total commitment Dickinson's persona has made with both body ('Say quick that I may dower thee / With last Delight I own!') and spirit. The echoes from *Cymbeline* reinforce the response of the poet's persona to her lover's doubt about that total commitment.

11.   The poem is dated by Johnson in 'Early 1862' and by Franklin in 'About 1862'; *Poems*, II, 390 and *Manuscript Books*, I, 354.

12.   For a valuable discussion of baptismal crownings, see Kantorowicz, *King's Two Bodies*, pp. 490–1.

13.   Lavinia Norcross wrote about her visiting niece, Emily Elizabeth Dickinson, on 20 May 1833: 'I suppose it will give you much joy to hear from us now as little Elizabeth (as we call her here) is now a member of our family . . . .' Leyda, *Years and Hours*, I, 21.

14.   For the connection between this letter (with the included poem 'Lad of Athens') and *Hamlet*, see Jack L. Capps, *Reading*, p. 64; Hyatt H. Waggoner has suggested that 'The "lad of Athens" is probably Dionysius the Areopagite, of whom we read in Acts 17:34 that he was one of those converted by Paul's preaching on Mars Hill in Athens'. Waggoner, *American Poets: From the Puritans to the Present* (Boston: Houghton, Mifflin Company, 1968), p. 203.

15.   Capps, *Reading*, p. 212.

16.   Sewall, *Lyman Letters*, p. 73; the following quotation is on the same page.

17.   Johnson and Franklin date this poem in about 1862; *Poems*, II, 445 and *Manuscript Books*, I, 308.

18.   For a different view of Dickinson's response to Biblical parable, see David Porter, *Dickinson: The Modern Idiom* (Cambridge, Mass.: Harvard Univ. Press, 1981), esp. pp. 167–79; Porter finds in the extreme compression and syntactical obscurity of Dickinson's idiom a 'divorce of language from the phenomenally experienced world [that] creates powerful effects characteristic of the extreme modernist sensibility' (p. 75); I offer another view of Dickinson's idiom in this section. I would urge that the powerful effects of her most fully realised poems – her parables of doubt and redemption – animate and dramatise religious questions of urgent concern to her time and to ours; her views of immortality (discussed at greater length in

Chapter Four) reflect and refract those of, among others, Wadsworth and Higginson.

19. W. O. E. Oesterley, *The Gospel Parables in the Light of Their Jewish Background* (London: Society for Promoting Christian Knowledge, 1936), p. 5; Dan Otto Via, Jr, *The Parables: Their Literary and Existential Dimension* (Philadelphia: Fortress Press, 1967).

20. Though I disagree with his conclusions, I am indebted in the following to Charles R. Anderson, *Stairway of Surprise*, pp. 42–6.

21. A psychological explanation of Dickinson's use of eating imagery in many poems is offered by Barbara Antonina Clarke Mossberg, *Emily Dickinson: When a Writer Is a Daughter* (Bloomington: Indiana Univ. Press, 1982), esp. pp. 135–46; Mossberg does not mention 'He ate and drank the precious Words – ' or 'A Word made Flesh is seldom' (discussed in my following paragraphs) – a poem that transforms John's doctrine of the Logos to convey her own religious vision.

22. A. M. Hunter, commentary on *The Gospel According to John* (Cambridge: Cambridge Univ. Press, 1965), p. 19.

23. Watts, *Psalms*, pp. 476–7.

24. In her extended discussion of 'A Word made Flesh is seldom', Shira Wolosky observes that 'The word that breathes distinctly is deathless and spiritual, not only like the Logos, but because of it'; but Wolosky sees in the closing lines evidence for the poet's view of a widening gulf: 'The Word no longer condescends to enter into the human world.' Wolosky, *Emily Dickinson: A Voice of War* (New Haven, Conn.: Yale Univ. Press, 1984), pp. 146, 148. I would suggest that the opening stanza offers intimations of condescension and the closing stanza the wish that these intimations be fulfilled – that God's condescension be as proximate and attainable as inspired earthly language.

25. Anderson, *Stairway of Surprise*, pp. 42, 44.

26. England, 'Emily Dickinson and Isaac Watts', in Martha Winburn England and John Sparrow, *Hymns Unbidden: Donne, Herbert, Blake, Emily Dickinson and the Hymnographers* (New York: The New York Public Library, 1966), p. 126.

27. Allen, Preface to *Psalms and Hymns for Public Worship* (Boston: Peirce, 1835), pp. iii–xxxi; the quoted statements are on pp. xvi–xvii, xviii–xix, xix, xxiii.

28. 'The Newest Poet', *London Daily News*, 2 January 1891; in *The Recognition of Emily Dickinson*, ed. Caesar R. Blake and Carlton F. Wells (Ann Arbor: Univ. of Michigan Press, 1968), p. 27.

29. For a recent valuable discussion of Watts's irregularities as a forerunner of Dickinson's, see Cristanne Miller, *Emily Dickinson: A Poet's Grammar* (Cambridge, Mass.: Harvard Univ. Press, 1987), pp. 141–3. Other useful commentaries on Watts's importance to Dickinson include James Davidson, 'Emily Dickinson and Isaac Watts', *The Boston Public Library Quarterly*, 6 (1954), 141–9; Johnson, *Emily Dickinson*, pp. 84–6; Anderson, *Stairway of Surprise*, pp. 24–7; Martha Winburn England, 'Emily Dickinson and Isaac Watts', in *Hymns Unbidden*, pp. 113–48; David Porter, *The Art of Emily Dickinson's Early Poetry*

(Cambridge, Mass. : Harvard Univ. Press, 1966), pp. 55–74; Brita Lindberg-Seyersted, *The Voice of the Poet: Aspects of Style in the Poetry of Emily Dickinson* (Cambridge, Mass. :Harvard Univ. Press, 1968), esp. pp. 129–31, 161–2; Porter, *Modern Idiom*, pp. 98–104; Wendy Martin, *An American Triptych: Anne Bradstreet, Emily Dickinson, Adrienne Rich* (Chapel Hill: Univ. of North Carolina Press, 1984), pp. 138–40; Wolosky, *Voice of War*, pp. 12–15, 23–4, 93–4; Shira Wolosky, 'Rhetoric or Not: Hymnal Tropes in Emily Dickinson and Isaac Watts', *New England Quarterly*, 61 (1988), 214–32.

30.   See England, 'Emily Dickinson and Isaac Watts', p. 113.

31.   Bingham, *Emily Dickinson's Home*, p. 35; for later family reminiscences involving recitations from Watts by Judge Lord and Lavinia Dickinson, see Barton Levi St Armand, *Soul's Society*, p. 158.

32.   Samuel M. Worcester, Preface to Watts, *Psalms*, pp. 5, 6; Worcester, Professor of Rhetoric at Amherst College, is quoting from a preface to an earlier edition by his father, the Reverend Dr. Samuel Worcester. His own preface is dated 'Amherst College, Jan. 20, 1834'. Worcester's observations reinforce Charles R. Anderson's suggestion that Dickinson's dashes seem to be 'an attempt to create a new system of musical notation for reading her verse'. (Anderson, *Stairway of Surprise*, p. 306). For an elaborate theory of Dickinson's punctuation as elocutionary symbols used in a standard rhetorical reader assigned to her at Amherst Academy, see Edith Wylder, *The Last Face: Emily Dickinson's Manuscripts* (Albuquerque: Univ. of New Mexico Press, 1971). For the view that Dickinson's punctuation had no special significance, see R. W. Franklin, *The Editing of Emily Dickinson: A Reconsideration* (Madison: Univ. of Wisconsin Press, 1967), esp. pp. 120–8.

33.   Watts, *Psalms*, p. 80.

34.   I am indebted to Thomas H. Johnson for his explanation of the word 'Checks' (*Poems*, II, 742); for a reading of the term as commercial metaphor, see George Monteiro, 'Love & Fame or What's a Heaven For?': Emily Dickinson's Teleology', *New England Quarterly*, 51 (1978), 108–10; Lindberg-Seyersted, *Voice of the Poet*, p. 70, in an otherwise valuable discussion of Dickinson's colloquial diction, mistakenly believes that the word *checks* is used by the poet to mean *railway tickets*.

35.   Watts, *Psalms*, p. 465.

36.   *The Complete Poems of Stephen Crane*, ed. Joseph Katz (Ithaca, N.Y.: Cornell Univ. Press, 1972), p. 94.

37.   Wolosky, *Voice of War*, pp. 76–7.

38.   Watts, *Psalms*, p. 548.

39.   Martha Dickinson Bianchi, *Emily Dickinson Face to Face: Unpublished Letters with Notes and Reminiscences* (Boston: Houghton Mifflin, 1932), p. 41, n. 1; Sewall, *Life*, II, 688–94 and 688, n. 15; Capps, *Reading*, pp. 61–2.

40.   Thomas à Kempis, *The Imitation of Christ* (London: Collins Clear-Type Press, [n.d.]), p. 114; the quoted words at the close of the following sentence are on p. 211.

41. Charles R. Anderson sees, in Dickinson's 'probing of the season's ambiguous appearance', a conflict in the mind of the poet over nature's message; but surely we are to learn from the undeceived bee to come as a child to this sacrament of celebration. See Anderson, *Stairway of Surprise*, pp. 145–9. E. Miller Budick finds in the poem 'the assertion of a clearly interpretable symbolic relationship between nature and Christianity' – but 'the burden of Dickinson's poem is not to confirm' this symbolic relationship but to call it into serious question. In support of this view, Budick points out that the speaker of the poem is 'by her own admission a child' too young for such sacramental rites. Budick, *Emily Dickinson and the Life of Language: A Study in Symbolic Poetics* (Baton Rouge: Louisiana State Univ. Press, 1985), pp. 55, 58.
42. Thomas à Kempis, *Imitation*, p. 133.
43. For valuable discussions of this subject, see Sewall, *Life*, II, 690–3; Eberwein, *Strategies of Limitation*, pp. 248–51; Dorothy Huff Oberhaus, '"Tender Pioneer": Emily Dickinson's Poems on the Life of Christ', *American Literature*, 59 (1987), 34–58.
44. Johnson and Franklin date the poem in about 1862; *Poems*, II, 423 and *Manuscript Books*, II, 708.
45. Cynthia Griffin Wolff suggests that, for Dickinson, 'The word "Crucifixion" becomes no more than a trope for extraordinary pain . . . .', Wolff, *Emily Dickinson*, p. 457.
46. Capps, *Reading*, p. 61.
47. Ibid.; *Imitation*, pp. 69–70. Richard B. Sewall cites similar passages and comments on their pervasiveness: '"Despise the world." "Fly the tumultuousness of the world as much as thou canst." "Take refuge within the closet of thine heart." These and similar exhortations echo and reecho throughout the *Imitation*' (*Life*, II, 689).
48. Browne, 'Christian Morals', Part 3, Section 9; in *Religio Medici* (Boston:Ticknor and Fields, 1862), p. 246; Capps, *Reading*, p. 67.
49. Browne, *Religo Medici*, Part 2, Sections 5 and 6, p. 129.
50. Johnson and Franklin date the poem in about 1862; *Poems*, I, 225 and *Manuscript Books*, I, 434. Jack L. Capps has pointed out the link between 'The Soul selects her own Society – ' and the views of Thomas à Kempis and Browne; Capps, *Reading*, 67–8.
51. Higginson, 'Letter to a Young Contributor', *Atlantic Monthly*, 9 (1862), 405.
52. For Browne's importance to Dickinson, see Herbert E. Childs, 'Emily Dickinson and Sir Thomas Browne', *American Literature*, 22 (1951), 455–65; Anderson, *Stairway of Surprise*, pp. 45–6, 55; Capps, *Reading*, pp. 46–8.
53. Browne, *Religio Medici*, Part 1, Section 15, p. 31.
54. *Poems*, II, 753.
55. Browne, *Religio Medici*, Part 1, Section 16, p. 32; for an extended discussion of 'Further in Summer than the Birds' (that finds in it a disclosure of 'our plight as being isolated from both nature and God'), see Brita Lindberg-Seyersted, *Voice of the Poet*, pp. 261–8.
56. Browne, *Religio Medici*, Part 1, Section 12, p. 26.

57. For a valuable discussion of the poem – and of Browne's importance to Dickinson, see Anderson, *Stairway of Surprise*, pp. 45–6.

58. Murray Roston, 'The "Doubting" Thomas', in *Approaches to Sir Thomas Browne*, ed. C. A. Patrides (Columbia: Univ. of Missouri Press, 1982), p. 80.

59. For the view that Dickinson's figurative expressions should not be taken literally and that her central emphasis was secular and aesthetic, see Charles R. Anderson, *Stairway of Surprise*, p. 46; that figurative expressions should not be taken literally is an unexceptionable position – but I would urge that Dickinson's life and art were inextricably linked to her lifelong struggle for religious belief.

60. Browne, *Religio Medici*, Part 1, Section 9, p. 141.

61. Louis L. Martz, *The Poem of the Mind: Essays on Poetry / English and American* (New York: Oxford Univ. Press, 1966), pp. 92–3, 98, 28. According to Greg Johnson, the variant 'Our faith' is a less hopeful phrase for 'it is by definition unchanging and cannot submit to regulation' (*Emily Dickinson: Perception and the Poet's Quest* [University: Univ. of Alabama Press, 1985], p. 372); Dickinson occasionally uses the term *faith* to convey orthodoxy ('"Faith" is a fine invention' [185]) – but it is more often used to represent a deep individual belief that we lose at our peril ('To lose one's faith – surpass / The loss of an Estate – ' [377]).

62. *The Works of George Herbert*, ed. T. E. Hutchinson (Oxford: Oxford Univ. Press, 1941), p. 12; the last two lines (of the quoted excerpt) are marked. See Capps, *Reading*, p. 69.

63. Dickinson's manuscript copy of Herbert's stanzas is reproduced in facsimile in Millicent Todd Bingham, *Emily Dickinson: A Revelation* (New York: Harper & Brothers, 1954), p. 108. In addition to the *Springfield Republican* publication of 'Mattens', the poem was also available to the poet in the family library copy of Chambers' *Cyclopaedia of English Literature*; see Capps, *Reading*, pp. 69, 68.

64. Ibid., p. 69.

65. *The Sacred Poets of England and America*, ed. Rufus W. Griswold (New York: D. Appleton & Company, 1850), p. 210; Capps, *Reading*, p. 68 calls attention to a copy of this anthology in the Dickinson family library.

66. See Johnson's note, *Poems*, III, 1079.

67. For Dickinson's involvement with Vaughan, see Capps, *Reading*, pp. 69–71, 139; see also Judith Banzer, '"Compound Manner": Emily Dickinson and the Metaphysical Poets', *American Literature*, 32 (1961), esp. 426–7, 429, 430–1.

68. 'An Elegie on the death of Mr. *R. W.* ', *The Complete Poetry of Henry Vaughan*, ed. French Fogle (New York: New York Univ. Press, 1965), pp. 68–71.

69. Louis L. Martz, *The Paradise Within: Studies in Vaughan, Traherne and Milton* (New Haven, Conn. :Yale Univ. Press, 1964), pp. 12–13.

70. Quoted in Banzer, '"Compound Manner"', p. 427; my following comparison with Dickinson's 'On a Columnar Self – ' draws on Banzer.

71. Johnson and Franklin date the poem in about 1863; *Poems*, II, 596 and

Manuscript Books, II, 870.

72.   Banzer, '"Compound Manner"', p. 427.

CHAPTER THREE: SINGING OFF CHARNEL STEPS: LESSONS FOR A PRECEPTOR

1.   For a valuable discussion of martial religious rhetoric in this period, see Shira Wolosky, *Voice of War*, esp. pp. 57–8.

2.   Watts, *Psalms*, p. 563.

3.   The index, prepared by Professor Samuel M. Worcester of Amherst College, is in ibid., pp. 20–36.

4.   Johnson dates the poem in about 1859; Franklin in about 1858. *Poems*, I, 105; *Manuscript Books*, I, 20.

5.   Johnson dates the poem in 1859; Franklin in about 1859. *Poems*, I, 53; *Manuscript Books*, I, 74.

6.   Wilbur, 'Sumptuous Destitution', in *Emily Dickinson: A Collection of Critical Essays*, ed. Richard B. Sewall (Englewood Cliffs, N.J.: Prentice-Hall, 1963), p. 132; for an illuminating discussion of Dickinson's conception of gain through loss, see Albert J. Gelpi, *Emily Dickinson: The Mind of the Poet* (Cambridge, Mass. : Harvard Univ. Press, 1965), pp. 69–72. Wolosky, *Voice of War*, pp. 84–5, emphasises Dickinson's 'disguised irony' in 'Success is counted sweetest'.

7.   Johnson and Franklin date this poem in about 1859; *Poems*, I, 90 and *Manuscript Books*, I, 92.

8.   Dahl, '"To Fight Aloud" and "The Charge of the Light Brigade": Dickinson on Tennyson', *New England Quarterly*, 52 (1979), 97.

9.   Leyda, *Years and Hours*, II, 26.

10.   Stearns's sermon was printed in the *Springfield Republican* of 13 July 1861; quoted in Wolosky, *Voice of War*, p. 52.

11.   See Johnson's note, *Letters*, II, 376; according to Johnson, the extract referring to the war was written after the death of Elizabeth Barrett Browning (29 June 1861).

12.   William Augustus Stearns, *Adjutant Stearns* (Boston: Sabbath School Society, 1862); quoted in St Armand, *Soul's Society*, pp. 112–13. Two copies of this volume, one of them inscribed to Edward Dickinson, are among the Dickinson books at Harvard (ibid., p. 330, n. 24).

13.   Dickinson enclosed, in her letter, a letter for Bowles to forward ('Will you be kind to *Austin* – again?'); Thomas Johnson suggests that Austin's name is used throughout 'as a cover' for her own. *Letters*, II, 399.

14.   St Armand, *Soul's Society*, pp. 107, 105, 107; Franklin has recently assigned the Master letter ('If you saw a bullet') to the summer of 1862. *Master Letters*, pp. 7–9.

15.   In an Epilogue to 'The Charge of the Heavy Brigade at Balaclava' (written shortly before his more famous poem about the Light Brigade), Tennyson presents a dialogue in verse in which he responds to the criticism that he was glorifying the barbarism of war. In it the

poet expresses hope for a future world of peace and love – but in
this imperfect world man must fight for peace, 'must combat might
with might, / Or Might would rule alone . . . '. The patriot-soldier
who bleeds in such a cause deserves to be memorialised in verse;
the poet who celebrates these heroes cannot share the dark view,
'in this lean age forlorn', that man's good and brave deeds have
no meaning beyond the grave. The patriot-poet's voice serves a
vital purpose: 'The song that nerves a nation's heart / Is in itself
a deed.' *The Complete Poetical Works of Tennyson*, ed. W. J. Rolfe
(Boston: Houghton Mifflin Company, 1898), pp. 510–11.

16. Quoted in St Armand, *Soul's Society*, p. 112.
17. Johnson and Franklin date this poem in about 1862; *Poems*, I, 330
and *Manuscript Books*, I, 408. According to Thomas Johnson (*Poems*,
I, 330), the poem was written 'almost certainly' on the occasion of
Frazar Stearns's death.
18. Ford, *Heaven Beguiles the Tired: Death in the Poetry of Emily Dickinson*
(University: Univ. of Alabama Press, 1966), pp. 133–4.
19. Johnson and Franklin date this poem in about 1862; *Poems*, I, 344 and
Manuscript Books, I, 534.
20. Howe, 'The Battle Hymn of the Republic', *Atlantic Monthly*, 9 (1862),
[145].
21. *Letters and Journals of Thomas Wentworth Higginson, 1846–1906*, ed.
Mary Thacher Higginson (New York: Negro Universities Press,
1969), p. 113.
22. Edelstein, *Strange Enthusiasm: A Life of Thomas Wentworth Higginson*
(New Haven, Conn. : Yale Univ. Press, 1968), pp. 247 and 274n.
23. Ibid., p. 252.
24. Ibid., pp. 255–6.
25. Wells, 'The Soul's Society: Emily Dickinson and Colonel Higginson',
in *Nineteenth-Century Women Writers of the English-Speaking World*,
p. 222.
26. St Armand, *Soul's Society*, pp. 199–200; for a valuable discussion of
Higginson's important influence on Dickinson's nature writings, see
pp. 183–8.
27. Higginson, 'Letter to a Young Contributor', p. 409.
28. Ibid., p. 403.
29. Ibid., pp. 410–11.
30. Higginson, *The Results of Spiritualism* (New York: S. T. Munson,
n.d.), pp. 6, 5; according to the title page, the lecture (delivered
on 6 March 1859) is 'Phonographically Reported'. Higginson had
delivered a similar lecture in New York four months earlier; see Ruth
Brandon, *The Spiritualists: The Passion for the Occult in the Nineteenth
and Twentieth Centuries* (New York: Alfred A. Knopf, 1983), pp. 39,
40, 289, nn. 41 and 44.
31. Higginson, 'Emily Dickinson's Letters', *Atlantic Monthly*, 68 (1891),
445.
32. Higginson, 'Ought Women to Learn the Alphabet?'*Atlantic Monthly*,
3 (1859), 149.
33. Higginson, 'Emily Dickinson's Letters', p. 445.

34. Ibid.
35. Leyda, *Years and Hours*, II, 71; the following reference (to a *Republican* item about Higginson on 6 February) is on p. 75.
36. [Higginson], 'The Procession of the Flowers', *Atlantic Monthly*, 10 (December 1862), 650.
37. Ibid., pp. 656, 655.
38. For valuable comments on the importance of 'The Procession of the Flowers' to Dickinson, see St Armand, *Soul's Society*, pp. 202, 204, 206, 340 n. 10.
39. Banzer, '"Compound Manner"', p. 27, refers to but does not quote from the stanzas reproduced in the *Republican*; my quotations are taken from *The Complete Poetry of Henry Vaughan*, p. 309.
40. Johnson and Franklin date this poem in about 1862; *Poems*, II, 529 and *Manuscript Books*, II, 562.
41. Johnson and Franklin date the poem in about 1862; *Poems*, I, 409 and *Manuscript Books*, I, 640. For valuable comments on this poem, see Wolosky, *Voice of War*, pp. 37, 38, 45.
42. Johnson and Franklin date the poem in about 1862; *Poems*, II, 492 and *Manuscript Books*, II, 786.
43. For a discussion of the ways in which 'The Civil War combined the cataclysm of fratricide with the upheaval of a religious schism' – and of 'My Portion is Defeat' – see Shira Wolosky, *Voice of War*, pp. 56–9; Wolosky finds a link between the 'scraps of Prayer' in the poem and the prayer Dickinson offered to Higginson when she first wrote to him at the front (pp. 56–7). St Armand discusses the popular and public sources for 'Dickinson's apotheosis of Frazar Stearns' and calls 'My Portion is Defeat' a compensation 'for her own obscure Antietams of the spirit' (*Soul's Society*, pp. 109–13).
44. For accounts of Higginson's war injury, see Edelstein, *Strange Enthusiasm*, p. 288, and Anna Mary Wells, *Dear Preceptor: The Life and Times of Thomas Wentworth Higginson* (Boston: Houghton Mifflin Company, 1963), pp. 177–8. Wells suggests (p. 178) that Higginson's severe incapacity and slow recovery after this engagement would be called in this century 'shell shock or combat neurosis'.
45. Leyda, *Years and Hours*, II, 82, dates the letter 'July?'1863.
46. Johnson and Franklin date the poem in about 1861; *Poems*, I, 205 and *Manuscript Books*, I, 200.
47. A stanza from a funeral hymn (Watts, *Psalms*, p. 761) is characteristic:

> Turn, mortal, turn! thy danger know:
> Where'er thy foot can tread,
> The earth rings hollow from below,
> And warns thee of her dead!

48. Cameron, *Lyric Time: Dickinson and the Limits of Genre* (Baltimore: The Johns Hopkins Univ. Press, 1979), pp. 106–7. Willis J. Buckingham has argued that Cameron's view blunts the point of the poem: 'The enlivening paradox in [Dickinson's] conception of death is that it can be unimaginably close while remaining unimaginable, and that

thinking about it balks thinking' ('Dickinson's "That After Horror – That 'Twas *Us*"', *Explicator*, 40 [Summer 1982], 34–5).

49. The last stanza (opening "Twould start them – ') is mistakenly omitted in the Johnson edition and appended to 'I tie my Hat – I crease my Shawl – ' (443); see Franklin, *The Editing of Emily Dickinson*, pp. 40–6. I have adopted Franklin's reconstruction of both these poems. No manuscript copy of the poem has survived but Franklin has demonstrated that it was copied on a leaf missing from Fascicle 29 – dated in about 1862; see ibid., pp. 46–7 and *Manuscript Books*, I, 534.

50. Shira Wolosky's reading of the poem (in Johnson's version) emphasises the religious dilemma as central to the poem (*Voice of War*, pp. 6–9); I would argue that this centrality is inextricably linked to the prospect and uncertainty of heavenly marriage. William H. Shurr sees the poem as a commentary on the dilemma of the two lovers confronting strong community disapproval; the bomb metaphor 'surely derives from conception ("we got"), gestation, and nursing' (*Marriage*, pp. 182–3).

51. This extract (the manuscript was destroyed) is assigned by Johnson to '1864?'because of the opening reference to the war and because Browning's *Dramatis Personae* was published in 1864. *Letters*, II, 436–7.

52. For a comprehensive account of Dickinson's eye troubles, see Sewall, *Life*, esp. II, 606–7, n. 9. John Cody has provided a psychoanalytical explanation in his *After Great Pain: The Inner Life of Emily Dickinson* (Cambridge, Mass. : The Belknap Press of Harvard Univ. Press, 1971), esp. pp. 415–24. More recently Martin B. Wand and Richard B. Sewall have offered evidence for the likelihood that Dickinson underwent surgery for *exotropia* (in lay terms, she was 'walleyed'); see '"Eyes Be Blind, Heart Be Still": A New Perspective on Emily Dickinson's Eye Problem', *New England Quarterly*, 52 (1979), 401–6; their evidence, based on an ophthalmological analysis of the only authentic photograph of Emily Dickinson known to exist, has been challenged by Mary Elizabeth Kromer Bernhard, 'A Response to "Eyes Be Blind, Heart Be Still"', *New England Quarterly*, 55 (1982), 112–14.

53. Thomas Johnson offers evidence that Sue forwarded her own copy of the poem to Samuel Bowles because he had admired it. *Poems*, II, 713.

54. Johnson, *Emily Dickinson*, p. 107; for a recent account of Higginson as uncomprehending and hostile, see Karl Keller, *The Only Kangaroo Among the Beauty: Emily Dickinson and America* (Baltimore: Johns Hopkins Univ. Press, 1979), esp. pp. 213–20; Cynthia Wolff, *Emily Dickinson*, pp. 252–9, portrays Dickinson's response to Higginson as ambivalent, playfully malicious, duplicitous.

55. Higginson, 'Emily Dickinson's Letters', p. 451.

56. I have found extremely valuable Karen Dandurand's discussion of the Dickinson-Higginson relationship; see Dandurand, *Why Dickinson Did Not Publish*, esp. pp. 147–58.

57.   Higginson's ambivalent response became, at least for a time, flip-
      pantly hostile after his second visit to Amherst and the poet's house
      (in December 1873); he wrote to his sisters: 'I saw my eccentric
      poetess Miss Emily Dickinson who never goes outside her father's
      grounds & sees only me & a few others . . . . I'm afraid [his wife]
      Mary's other remark "Oh why do the insane so cling to you?"still
      holds. ' Johnson, *Letters*, II, 518–19.
58.   For Higginson's involvement with spiritualism, see my Chapter
      Four, section 1.
59.   Higginson, *Malbone: An Oldport Romance* (Boston: Fields, Osgood &
      Co., 1869); my quotation is from the magazine version that preceded
      the appearance of the book, *Atlantic Monthly*, 23 (1869), 1.
60.   Johnson and Franklin date the poem in about 1863; *Poems*, II, 565 and
      Manuscript Books, II, 896.
61.   Higginson, 'Malbone', p. 663.
62.   Higginson, 'Decoration', in *The Afternoon Landscape: Poems and Trans-
      lations* (New York: Longmans, Green and Co. , 1889), pp. 24–5; the
      poem is reproduced in *Poems*, III, 961.
63.   A sentence in Dickinson's letter ('My Brother and Sister thank you
      for remembering them') suggests that she is writing in response to
      a condolence letter from him.
64.   Johnson has suggested that Dickinson's comment on 'Immortality'
      might refer to the poem '"Faithful to the end" Amended' – enclosed
      in her preceding letter to Higginson; *Letters*, II, 552.
65.   In a letter to her friend Joseph Lyman, Emily Dickinson tells of
      her father occasionally confiding to her his sense of alienation
      from others: 'Father says in fugitive moments when he forgets the
      barrister & lapses into the man, says that his life has been passed in
      a wilderness or on an island – of late he says on an island. ' Sewall,
      Lyman Letters, p. 70.
66.   Leyda, *Years and Hours*, I, 328.
67.   Bingham, *Ancestor's Brocades*, pp. 129–30; for a valuable account of
      Dickinson's relationship with her father – and of her redaction of
      Higginson's 'Decoration', see Sewall, *Life*, esp. I, 71–3.
68.   Edelstein, *Strange Enthusiasm*, pp. 336–7; Higginson's paternalistic
      view of the woman's rights advocate Lucy Stone anticipates the
      language of his diary entry about his wife: [Lucy Stone is] one
      of the noblest & gentlest persons whom I know . . . – & her deli-
      cious voice; I think the very sweetest voice I have ever heard
      in public speaking.' Ibid., pp. 350–1. For a valuable discussion
      of Higginson's ambivalence about Dickinson (that emphasises the
      poet's posturing as a pupil), see Martha Nell Smith, '"Rowing in
      Eden"', esp. pp. 309–36; Smith's quoted words are on page 312. In
      her discussion of the relationship, Barbara Mossberg has suggested
      that Higginson's 'fatherlike obtuseness about her poetic skills is a
      function of Dickinson's sham as a dutiful daughter'; see Mossberg,
      When a Writer, p. 91.
69.   Higginson, 'Emily Dickinson's Letters', pp. 455–6.
70.   Chambers' *Cyclopaedia of English Literature*, in the Dickinson family

library, would have made Marvell's poem available to her; there
is no evidence that Dickinson read and was echoing the poem –
but, at the least, Higginson's admiration for Marvell helps explain
his admiration for Dickinson's letter. (I am indebted to Joseph
Lease for calling my attention to the Dickinson–Marvell parallel.)
In this same letter to Higginson, Dickinson explicitly quotes a line
(somewhat inaccurately) from Vaughan's 'They are all gone into
the world of light!': "Twas noting some such Scene made Vaughn
humbly say "My Days that are at best but dim and hoary" –
' (L653).

71. Wells, *Dear Preceptor*, pp. 261–2; in her congratulatory letter, written
after the birth of Higginson's second child, Dickinson wrote: 'I
am very grateful for the delight to you and Mrs Higginson –
I had thought of your future with soft fear – I am glad it has
come – ' (L728)

72. Dickinson's second letter to Sue after Gilbert's death consisted of this
quatrain: 'Climbing to reach the costly Hearts / To which he gave the
worth, / He broke them, fearing punishment / He ran away from
Earth – ' (L870)

73. For Higginson's illness, see Johnson, *Letters*, III, 905.

74. Wells, 'Emily Dickinson and Colonel Higginson', p. 229.

75. Peggy Anderson, 'Biblical Influence on Emily Dickinson', p. 9.

76. My account draws on Wells, *Dear Preceptor*, pp. 370–1; Leyda, *Years
and Hours*, II, 474–6. Several days after the funeral, Harriet Jameson,
a neighbor who occasionally corresponded with the poet, reported
to her son that the quotation from First Corinthians ('on putting off
the earthly and putting on immortality') was Dickinson's favorite
passage from the Scriptures. Ibid., p. 475.

77. Higginson, *The Afternoon Landscape*, p. 58; for the link between 'Astra
Castra' and Dickinson, see Edelstein, *Strange Enthusiasm*, p. 345;
Sewall, *Life*, II, 575–6.

78. Higginson, 'An Open Portfolio', *Christian Union*, 42 (25 September
1890), 393. It is noteworthy that, in this instance – though he regu-
larises Dickinson's punctuation and capitalisation (the thirty-two
word manuscript poem has eighteen dashes and twenty capitals)
– Higginson altered none of the poet's words; for Dickinson's punctuation and capitalisation of the poem, see Franklin, *Editing*, p. 128.

79. Wadsworth, *Sermons* ([1869]; 1883), pp. 241, 252.

80. Bingham, *Ancestor's Brocades*, pp. 34–5.

81. Higginson, 'An Open Portfolio', p. 393.

82. In our time, David Porter has found in 'Departed to the Judgment' a
bewildering compression in which transitive and intransitive words
are collapsed, a crucial subject noun omitted – and a prevailing
fragmentation that adds up to 'a kind of closet language'; this
fragmentation (here and throughout the Dickinson canon), Porter
suggests, 'comes from the absence of an abiding life-centering angle
of vision in the poet's mind' (*Modern Idiom*, pp. 53, 115–16, 144).

83. Wells, *Dear Preceptor*, pp. 239–40; Dandurand, 'Why Dickinson Did
Not Publish', pp. 164, 167.

84. Higginson, 'An Open Portfolio', pp. 392, 393.
85. Anna Mary Wells has argued that Higginson was strongly on the side of 'Emily in her "so to speak unregenerate form" against the solid majority that believed she could be improved'; Higginson worked with the transcriptions prepared by Mabel Loomis Todd – and yielded to the pressures of Arlo Bates of Roberts Brothers, who complained of Dickinson's 'extraordinary crudity of workmanship' (*Dear Preceptor*, pp. 278–9). Franklin has disputed this claim, pointing out that Higginson's acceptance of Dickinson in her 'unregenerate form' refers to his interest in her in 1862 – not to his editorial practice; both editors must share the responsibility for smoothing away the rough places – and it was Higginson who was largely responsible for titling the poems (*Editing*, pp. 22–6). Martha Nell Smith has put the chief blame for the editorial changes on Higginson – changes that vitiate Dickinson's force as an intensely feminine (rather than genteel and ladylike) poet ('"Rowing in Eden"', esp. pp. 383–402). For a discussion of the enormous problems that must confront the editor of an ideal reader's edition of Dickinson's poems, see Franklin, *Editing*, pp. 115–43.
86. Higginson, 'An Open Portfolio', p. 393. Despite his refusal to count the syllables, Higginson altered the poem to a degree that, according to Martha Nell Smith, alters its meaning; Higginson's alteration of punctuation and a word ('the grammatically offensive "Themself" to "the Two"') emphasises a conventionally Christian interpretation ('"Rowing in Eden"', pp. 391–3). Whether or not he misinterpreted the poem, Higginson's response to it was unconventional: He was reminded of Blake and reacted to the poem in the way Dickinson reacted to a true poem, physically.

CHAPTER FOUR: NATURE'S HAUNTED HOUSE: 'CALLED BACK'

1. Russell M. and Clare R. Goldfarb, *Spiritualism and Nineteenth-Century Letters* (Rutherford, N. J. : Fairleigh Dickinson Univ. Press, 1978), pp. 38–9.
2. According to Jon Butler, 'Higginson scholars have had little to say about Higginson's spiritualism and its effect on his life and work'; Butler, 'The Dark Ages of American Occultism, 1760–1848', in *The Occult in America: New Historical Perspectives*, ed. Howard Kerr and Charles L. Crow (Urbana: Univ. of Illinois Press, 1983), p. 78, n. 30.
3. Edelstein, *Strange Enthusiasm*, p. 130; in Newburyport, Higginson had defended the right of a medium to practice against the harassment of the town government (ibid.). St Armand has discussed this and other episodes concerning Higginson's involvement with spiritualism; see his 'Veiled Ladies: Dickinson, Bettine, and Transcendental Mediumship', *Studies in the American Renaissance* (1987), pp. 5–6.
4. The affidavit is reproduced in Emma Hardinge [Britten], *Modern*

American Spiritualism ([1869]); New Hyde Park, N. Y. : University Books, 1970), pp. 183–5; see also Howard Kerr, *Mediums, and Spirit-Rappers, and Roaring Radicals: Spiritualism in American Literature, 1850–1900* (Urbana: Univ. of Illinois Press, 1972), pp. 101–2; Edelstein, *Strange Enthusiasm*, p. 130; St Armand, 'Veiled Ladies', p. 5.

5. Higginson, *Results of Spiritualism*, pp. 6, 5; according to the title page, the lecture was delivered on 6 March 1859. Higginson had delivered a similar lecture four months earlier; see Ruth Brandon, *Spiritualists*, pp. 39, 40, 289, nn. 41 and 44. For a recent discussion of Higginson's lecture, see St Armand, 'Veiled Ladies', pp. 6–7; St Armand suggests that Dickinson may have read the lecture and that it 'might well have shaped her own subtle fusion of nature worship and occult sensitivity into the hybrid attitude I have called Transcendental Mediumship' (p. 7).

6. Higginson, *Results of Spiritualism*, pp. 14–15.

7. Ibid. , pp. 16, 17–18.

8. Johnson dates this version of the poem in early summer, 1861; *Poems*, I, 152. For an account of the several versions of this poem, see ibid., pp. 152–5.

9. St Armand, *Soul's Society*, p. 23; Eberwein, *Strategies*, p. 132.

10. Higginson, 'An Open Portfolio', p. 393. Jane Donahue Eberwein (*Strategies*, p. 132) somewhat inaccurately says that Higginson 'later chose the 1859 fascicle version for his *Christian Union* article rather than the one she sent him'. Higginson prints the 1859 version as the one the poet finally chose – and he then prints, with praise, the second stanza of the 1861 version sent to him by Dickinson.

11. Johnson and Franklin date the poem in about 1862; *Poems*, I, 322 and *Manuscript Books*, I, 262.

12. For a valuable discussion of Dickinson's satiric use of a child persona's vision of heaven (linking it to Huck Finn's, in this and other poems), see Jane Donahue Eberwein, *Strategies*, pp. 234–5; the quoted passage is from *The Portable Mark Twain*, ed. Bernard DeVoto (New York: Viking Press, 1946), p. 196.

13. Higginson, *Results of Spiritualism*, pp. 16, 17, 20.

14. Kerr, *Mediums*, p. 179.

15. Higginson, *Results of Spiritualism*, pp. 16, 17, 20.

16. French had lived as a boy in Amherst and was a friend of the Norcross cousins; *Letters*, III, 282.

17. Higginson, *Results of Spiritualism*, pp. 14–15, 20.

18. Johnson and Franklin date the poem in about 1861; *Poems*, I, 202 and *Manuscript Books*, I, 334.

19. Kerr, *Mediums*, pp. 13–14; for Stowe's involvement, see ibid., esp. pp. 110, 162, 178.

20. Wadsworth, *Sermons* ([1869]; 1883), pp. 231, 231–2.

21. Ibid., pp. 237–8.

22. Ibid., pp. 232–4.

23. Ibid., pp. 235, 238–9.

24. Ibid., pp. 244–5.

25. Wadsworth, *Sermons* (1882), pp. 12, 13, 21–2.
26. Johnson dates the poem in early 1862, Franklin in about 1862; *Poems*, I, 269 and *Manuscript Books*, I, 408.
27. Wadsworth, *Sermons* ([1869]; 1883), pp. 239, 238.
28. For an example of Wadsworth's 'roguish' wit, see Sewall, *Life*, II, 455; an obituary notice in the *Presbyterian* for 8 April 1882, pays tribute to the minister's 'keen satire' (p. 10, column 3). A Resolution of the Calvary Church, San Francisco (appended to *Funeral Services*), praises Wadsworth's tolerance toward differing views (p. 30).
29. Johnson and Franklin date this poem in about 1862; *Poems*, II, 481 and *Manuscript Books*, II, 760.
30. The quoted words by Vaughan are from 'The Retreate', *Complete Poetry*, p. 170; the lines from Herbert's 'Death' is in *Works*, p. 186. For a view of "Twas a Long Parting – ' that emphasises its sentimentality and conventionality, see David Porter, *Modern Idiom*, pp. 220–1.
31. Hawthorne, *The American Notebooks*, Centenary Edition, ed. Claude M. Simpson (Columbus: Ohio State Univ. Press, 1972), p. 429.
32. Wadsworth, *An Address Delivered in Calvary Church* (San Francisco: H. H. Bancroft & Company, 1865), pp. 9–11; Wadsworth's funeral address was delivered on 21 October 1865.
33. Wadsworth, *Sermons* ([1869]; 1883), pp. 56–7.
34. Moshe Greenberg, 'Job', in *The Literary Guide to the Bible*, ed. Robert Alter and Frank Kermode (Cambridge, Mass.: The Belknap Press of Harvard Univ. Press, 1987), p. 297.
35. Wadsworth, *Sermons* (1882), pp. 37–9.
36. Ibid. , pp. 158, 159, 163, 167–9. Barton Levi St Armand has called attention to another Wadsworth sermon, 'The Treasures of Wisdom', in which veil imagery is used to emphasise our proximity to the other world. In it, the minister urges those who have been bereaved to 'look up from the grave's black shadows, to the radiant shapes that go by, behind the half-parted veil. You can almost see the beloved forms – almost hear the clear voices. And when the veil parts, and those clouds dissolve, ye shall walk with them in white robes, and be satisfied' ('Veiled Ladies', pp. 21–2).
37. Johnson and Franklin date the poem in about 1861; *Poems*, I, 185 and *Manuscript Books*, I, 258.
38. Wadsworth, *Sermons* (1882), p. 168.
39. *The Works of John Ruskin*, Library Edition, ed. E. T. Cook and Alexander Wedderburn (London: George Allen, 1903–1912), III, 75–76 n. 1; the quoted passage is from the draft version of a passage in *Modern Painters*, chapter 4, 'Of Turnerian Mystery: – First, As Essential', ibid., p. 75.
40. Ibid., p. 308.
41. That horror was conveyed in numerous letters to Charles Eliot Norton, his closest American friend, and in an 1865 lecture on war to the recruits at the Royal Military Academy, Woolwich; see Joan Abse, *John Ruskin: The Passionate Moralist* (London: Quartet Books, 1980), pp. 186–7, 188, 202.
42. Ruskin, 'The Mystery of Life and Its Arts', a lecture added to *Sesame*

and Lilies in 1871; quoted in *The Genius of John Ruskin*, ed. John D. Rosenberg, Riverside Edition (Boston: Houghton Mifflin Company, 1963), pp. 324–5.

43. Ruskin, *Fors Clavigera*; quoted in Raymond E. Fitch, *The Poison Sky: Myth and Apocalypse in Ruskin* (Athens: Ohio Univ. Press, 1982), p. 6.

44. St Armand, *Soul's Society*, p. 233; for a valuable discussion of Ruskin's influence on Dickinson, see pp. 219–59 passim.

45. Johnson and Franklin date the poem in about 1861; *Poems*, I, 209 and *Manuscript Books*, I, 258.

46. I am indebted to William R. Sherwood, *Circumference and Circumstance*, p. 207, for his explication of the word *Menagerie* in the poem. Charles R. Anderson seems to me to misread this poem when he suggests that 'their Competeless Show' refers back to 'My Splendors' – that is, her poems; he finds, in stanza two, that 'She lives on for a few centuries through her poems, for which she claims the kind of immortality possible to art' (*Stairway of Surprise*, pp. 52–4). For refutations of Anderson's reading, see Sherwood, *Circumference and Circumstance*, pp. 206–7 and Greg Johnson, *Perception and the Poet's Quest*, p. 197, n. 40.

47. G. Johnson, *Perception and the Poet's Quest*, p. 40.

48. Higginson, 'Snow', *Atlantic Monthly*, 9 (February 1862), 189.

49. Higginson, 'A Shadow', *Atlantic Monthly*, 26 (July 1870), 4.

50. Higginson, 'The Haunted Window', *Atlantic Monthly*, 19 (April 1867); the quoted passages are on pp. 434 and 435.

51. St Armand, *Soul's Society*, p. 287.

52. Higginson, 'In a Wherry', *Atlantic Monthly*, 29 (February 1872), 167.

53. For a cogent summary of Hawthorne's importance to Higginson, see James W. Tuttleton, *Thomas Wentworth Higginson* (Boston: Twayne Publishers, 1978), pp. 138–9; the quoted words from 'The Haunted Window'are on p. 437.

54. Higginson, 'The Haunted Window', p. 436.

55. Eberwein, *Strategies of Limitation*, p. 154.

56. Johnson dates the poem in about 1864, Franklin in about 1864–1865; *Poems*, II, 704 and *Manuscript Books*, II, 1032.

57. Wadsworth, *Sermons* (1882), p. 106; Mary Elizabeth Barbot has called attention to this and other similarities between passages in Wadsworth's sermons and Dickinson's poems ('Emily Dickinson Parallels', pp. 689–92).

58. Johnson dates the poem in about 1883; *Poems*, III, 1098.

59. D'Avanzo, '"Came a Wind Like a Bugle": Dickinson's Poetic Apocalypse', *Renascence*, 17 (Fall 1964), 29–31; D'Avanzo (p. 29, n. 2) takes exception to Anderson's view that the poem has only 'faint' Biblical allusions.

60. Anderson, *Stairway of Surprise*, p. 140.

61. Hawthorne, *The Blithedale Romance and Fanshawe*, Centenary Edition, ed. William Charvat and others (Columbus: Ohio State Univ. Press, 1964), pp. 200–2.

62. Ibid., p. 199.

63. For an explanatory reference to the fluids of Mesmer and

Reichenbach, see Janet Oppenheim, *The Other World: Spiritualism and Psychical Research in England, 1850–1914* (Cambridge: Cambridge Univ. Press, 1985), pp. 218–19; Beecher's negative response to spiritualism (and his later conversion to it) is described in Howard Kerr, *Mediums*, pp. 13–14.

64.   R. Laurence Moore, *In Search of White Crows: Spiritualism, Parapsychology, and American Culture* (New York: Oxford Univ. Press, 1977), pp. 49–50.

65.   Hitchcock, *Reminiscences of Amherst College* (Northhampton, Mass.: Bridgman & Childs, 1863), pp. 291–2.

66.   Sewall, *Life*, II, 342–48 *passim*; Dickinson's poem, 'The Chemical conviction', is dated by Johnson and Franklin in about 1864 (*Poems*, II, 692 and *Manuscript Books*, II, 1076).

67.   Hitchcock, 'Revelation Illustrated by Science', in *The Religion of Geology and Its Connected Sciences* ([1851] Boston: Crosby, Nichols, Lee & Company, 1860), pp. 7–8; this 1860 edition is identical with that of 1851, but adds one lecture, 'Synoptical View of the Bearings of Geology Upon Religion'. David Porter, *Modern Idiom*, refers to 'The Chemical conviction' as 'pointed satire' (p. 175).

68.   For the controversy that *The Religion of Geology* (1851) aroused, see Hitchcock's preface to the edition of 1859 [1860], pp. xiv-xv.

69.   Hitchcock's lecture, included in the 1851 edition of *The Religion of Geology*, seems to have been delivered no earlier than 1850 for it makes extensive references to the translation by William Gregory of Baron von Reichenbach's *Researches on Magnetism . . . in their Relations to the Vital Force* (London: Taylor, Walton and Maberly, 1850); see my following paragraphs for Hitchcock's discussion of Reichenbach.

70.   Hitchcock, *Religion of Geology*, p. 409.

71.   Ibid., p. 410.

72.   Ibid., pp. 424–5.

73.   Johnson and Franklin date the poem in about 1861; *Poems*, I, 217 and *Manuscript Books*, I, 226.

74.   Ward, *The Capsule of the Mind: Chapters in the Life of Emily Dickinson* (Cambridge, Mass.: The Belknap Press of Harvard Univ. Press, 1961), pp. 55–6; the ghostly presences, David Porter believes, may be 'the poetic impulse personified' (*Early Poetry*, p. 118).

75.   Hitchcock, *Religion of Geology*, p. iv.

76.   See Sewall, *Life*, II, 348.

77.   Johnson and Franklin date the poem in about 1862; *Poems*, I, 364 and *Manuscript Books*, II, 786.

78.   Louis L. Martz, *The Poetry of Meditation: A Study in English Religious Literature of the Seventeenth Century* (New Haven, Conn.: Yale Univ. Press, 1962), p. 214.

79.   The first message flashed over Samuel F. B. Morse's newly invented electromagnetic telegraph, in 1844, was 'What hath God wrought?' For details about this new development in communication in the years before and during the war, see John Wilson Townsend, *The Life of James Francis Leonard*, Filson Club Publications Number 24,

Part One (Louisville, Ky.: John P. Morton & Company, 1909), pp. 11–12, 47.

80. For a discussion of Hitchcock's influence on 'They put Us far apart – ' and other poems, see David H. Watters, 'Emerson, Dickinson, and the Atomic Self', *Emily Dickinson Bulletin*, Number 32 (Second Half 1977), pp. 129–32.

81. Johnson and Franklin date the poem in about 1862; *Poems*, II, 470 and *Manuscript Books*, I, 456.

82. Hitchcock, *Religion of Geology*, pp. 427, 425.

83. William Dean Howells, *The Undiscovered Country* (Boston: Houghton, Mifflin and Company, 1880), p. 238; for Dickinson's familiarity with Howells' novel, see her letters to Fanny Boltwood and Judge Lord (L629 and L752).

84. Elizabeth Stuart Phelps, 'What Did She See With?' *Atlantic Monthly*, 18 (August 1866), 151–3; according to Phelps, the story was 'a fictitious narrative of certain psychical phenomena occuring [sic] in Connecticut, and known to me, at first hand, to be authentic'. Quoted in Lori Duin Kelly, *The Life and Works of Elizabeth Stuart Phelps, Victorian Feminist Writer* (Troy, N.Y.: The Whitston Publishing Company, 1983), p. 3.

85. Hugh Conway (pseud. of Frederick John Fargus), *Called Back* (New York: Henry Holt and Company, 1884); Mabel Loomis Todd found the novel 'a singular & somewhat morbid story' – and seems to have loaned or given it to the poet during a visit to the Homestead on 4 November 1884. See Leyda, *Years and Hours*, II, 431, 435.

86. Conway, *Called Back*, p. 133.

87. For the view that the text of Dickinson's letter to her Norcross cousins was probably 'a playful echo of the title of [Conway's book]', see Jerome Loving, *Emily Dickinson: The Poet on the Second Story* (Cambridge: Cambridge Univ. Press, 1986), p. 14; Loving sees Dickinson's life as an escape from life: 'It was better to remain back with the "mind alone" than to follow the "harmony" of the body to the end' (p. 18). Cynthia Griffin Wolff has expressed a different view: 'Dickinson had read Hugh Conway's sentimental, spiritual novel, *Called Back*, and this note [to the Norcross cousins] was an expression of confidence about the realm that awaited her' (*Emily Dickinson*, p. 534). Susan Dickinson seems to have interpreted Dickinson's two-word letter in a similarly serious way. In 1891, she submitted for publication in the *Independent* her autograph copy of a poem about a close encounter with death ('Just lost, when I was saved!' [160]) and gave it the title "Called Back"; see *Poems*, I, 117. The poem was also given this title by Higginson and Todd when they included it in their edition of *Poems*, Second Series (1891).

88. *The Complete Works of Ralph Waldo Emerson*, Concord Edition (Boston: Houghton Mifflin and Company, 1903), VI, 313, 325.

89. Gelpi, *Mind of the Poet*, p. 54. Compare Carol Johnson's observation about Donne's religious uncertainty: 'Doubt is never with Donne the abdication of reason, but the incitement to reason' (*Reason's Double Agent* [Chapel Hill: Univ. of North Carolina Press, 1966], p. 51).

Index of Poems

The Index of Poems (by first lines) is arranged in a word–by–word alphabetical order. Poem numbers assigned by Johnson are given in parentheses. Entries in **bold** type indicate quotation and commentary. No attempt is made to reproduce the exact punctuation and capitalisation of these first lines as they appear in the text.

157

General Index

Entries in **bold** type indicate extended commentary.